ISBN 960-7310-69-1

BY S. VLASTOU

COPYRIGHT:
ADDRESS: I. MATHIOULAKIS & Co
ANDROMEDAS 1 VYRONAS 162 31
TEL. 7661351 - 7227229
ATHENS - GREECE
TRANSLATOR:

TABLE OF CONTENTS

ΑΝΤΙΠΡΟΣΩΠΟΣ ΚΡΗΤΗΣ
ΚΡΗΤΙΚΟ ΠΡΑΚΤΟΡΕΙΟ ΔΙΑΝΟΜΩΝ Ε.Π.Ε.
715 00 ΕΣΤΑΥΡΩΜΕΝΟΣ - ΗΡΑΚΛΕΙΟ
ΤΗΛ. 081 - 251.217

VITAMINS

Vitamins are substances indispensable, for the development of our body.

Because every kind of vitamin feeds and is needed for some organ of the body, you must eat of all kinds of food, to absorb as much as pos sible all the miscellaneous vitamins.

The vitamins separate into: A, B, C and D.

Vitamin A.

Endives
Apricots
Butter
Milk
Plums
Sea Food

Carrots Tomatoes
Pumpkins Beets
Egg Yolk Peaches
Cabbage Liver (pork or veal)
Lettuce String beans
Peas

Vitamin B.

Oat
Sugar
Chestnuts
Pork heart
Chicken
Cauliflower
Pork Meat
Veal

Barley Pork liver
Bier Yeast Dried Figs
Mushrooms Lentils
Banana Dates
Pork or Seep Rinds Fishes
Potatoes Wheaten bread
Radishes
Rice

Vitamin C.

Cucumbers
Pears
Plums
Walnuts
Chestnuts
Cherries
Meat
Cauliflower
Fresh beans

Onions Dandelions
Cabbage Celery
Lemons Beets
Apples Garlic
Fresh peas Spinach
Pork brain Asparagus
Tomatoes Grapes
Oranges Green beans
Leeks

Vitamin D.

Eggs
Butter
Oats
Cow milk
Mushrooms
Mussels

Bovine brain Eel
Tunna fish
Herring
Sardines
Mackerels
Salmon

CALORIES

By calories, we mean, the value of food to either produce energy or heat for our bodies. Calories are defined by units.

Calories board at 100 grams or 4 0Z. Vegetables.

100grams or 4 0Z		Kind calories	
100gr. or	4 0Z	Artichokes	7
" "		Asparagus	9
" "		Beet roots	44
" "		Carrots	23
" "		Celery roots	14
" "		Celery	8
" "		Mushrooms	13
" "		White raw cabbage	20
" "		Red " "	20
" "		Green boiled "	9
" "		White beans	93
" "		Green "	7
" "		Lentils	96
" "		Lettuce	12
" "		Corn	123
" "		Turnips	14
" "		Raw Onions	23
" "		Boiled "	13
" "		Peas	52
" "		Leeks	24
" "		Potatoes	76
" "		Raw Cauliflower	13
" "		Boiled "	9
" "		Cucumbers	13
" "		Pumpkins	12
" "		Endive	9
" "		Spinach	30
" "		Fried potatoes	264
" "		Potatoes chips	326
" "		Radishes	15
" "		Tomatoes	12
" "		Tomato juice	671

Fruits			
100grams	or 4 0Z		Kind calories
100gr.	or 4 OZ	Fresh apricots	25
"	"	Dry	182
"	"	Apricots preserve	106
"	"	Fresh Pineapple	46
"	"	Tangerine	23
"	"	Melon	15
"	"	Olives	82
"	"	Orange	26
"	Pineapple preserve		77
"	"	Banana	47
"	"	Cherries	41
"	"	Dates	213
"	"	Fresh Figs	41
"	"	Dried	213
"	"	Strawberries	26
"	"	Gooseberries	15
"	"	Plums Dried	161
"	"	Grapefruit	11
"	"	Water Melon	11
"	"	Fresh peach	32
"	"	Peach preserve	87
"	"	Apple	35
"	"	Plums	36
"	"	White grapes	63
"	"	Black "	51
"	"	Raisins	250

Nuts			
100grams	or 4 0Z		Kind calories
100gr.	or 4 OZ		Almonds 565
"	"	Chestnuts	170
"	"	Walnuts	525
"	"	Hazelnuts	380

Meats and Poultry
Cooked with out fat

100grams	or 4 OZ	Kind calories	
100gr.	or 4 OZ		Lamb leg 266
" "		Lamb roast	192
" "		Beef steak	168
" "		Pork roast	286
" "		Roast veal	230
" "		Kidneies	90
" "		Liver	153
" "		Duck	339
" "		Turkey	140
" "		Goose	319
" "		Chicken	145
" "		Rabbit	179
" "		Cornbeef	217
" "		Sausages	318
" "		Salami	491

Fish

100grams	or 4 OZ	Kind calories	
100gr.	or 4 OZ		Eel 200
" "		Bass	91
" "		Cod-fish	86
" "		Sturgeon	83
" "		Flatfish	90
" "		Stockfish	111
" "		Herring	135
" "		Tongue	93
" "		Sword fish	79
" "		Mullet	85
" "		Fresh Sardines	188
" "		Sardines preserved	334
" "		Smoked Salmon	142
" "		Fresh Salmon	160
" "		Tuna fish Fresh	127
" "		Tuna fish preserved	289
" "		Trout	89
" "		Caviar	273
" "		Sturgeon eggs	115
" "		Crab	93
" "		Shrimp	96
" "		Oysters	80
" "		Lobster	87
" "		Mussels	72

Butter - Eggs - Cheese - Oil

100grams	or 4 OZ	Kind calories
100gr.	or 4 OZ	Butter 740
" "	Milk cream	447
" "	Egg	147
" "	White cheese	90
" "	Brie	271
" "	Graviera	391
" "	Parmezana	408
" "	RoqueFort	405
" "	Milk	65
" "	Skim Milk	33
" "	Yogurt	75
" "	Yogurt without butter	54
" "	Oil	900
" "	Margarine	730
" "	Mayonnaise	718

Cereals/Grains

100grams	or 4 OZ	Kind calories
100gr.	or 4 OZ	Flour 337
" "	Toast bread	362
" "	Corn	354
" "	Bread	290
" "	Pastries	117
" "	Rice	360
" "	Semolina	350
" "	Biscuits and cakes	300-500
" "	Candy	327-430
" "	Chocolate	530
" "	Marmalade	260
" "	Ice creams	170
" "	Honey	288
" "	Sugar	394

Drinks

100grams	or 4 OZ	Kind calories
100gr.	or	4 OZ Chocolate 366
" "	Liquer	255
" "	Porto	157
" "	Ouzo	222
" "	Wine	66-71

Conversion from grams to pound (Lb) and Ounce (OZ) is approximate.

1 pound (Lb) is equivalent with 454 grams

1	"	"	"	"	16 ounces (OZ)	
1	ounce (OZ)	"		"	28	grams
2	ounces (OZ)	"		"	56	"
3	"	"	"	"		85 "
4	"	"	"	"		115 "
5	"	"	"	"		144 "
6	"	"	"	"		172 "
7	"	"	"	"		201 "
8	"	"	"	"		230 "
9	"	"	"	"		259 "
10	"	"	"	"		288 "
11	"	"	"	"		316 "
36	"	"	"	"		1 kilo

Conversion of the table spoonful, and cup, to grams

1	cup water	is 208	grams,	or 7 OZ
1	"	olive oil	is 192 ",	or 6 OZ
1	"	butter	is 224",	or 8 OZ
1	"	Sugar	is 208",	or 7 OZ
1	"	Flour	is 128",	or 4 OZ
1	"	Sugar flour	is 135",	or 5 OZ
1	"	Rice is 208	",	or 7 OZ
1	Tablespoonful Rice	is 16",		or 1/2 OZ
1	"	Sugar	is 16 ",	or 1/2 OZ
1	"	Flour	is 16 ",	or 1/2 OZ

OVEN TEMPERATURES

Very slow	250Fo		120Co	1/4 gas regulo
Slow	300Fo	150Co	1	"
Moderately Slow	325Fo	162Co	2	"
Moderate	350Fo	177Co	3	"
Moderate hot	375Fo	190Co	4	"
Hot	400Fo	204Co	5	"
hot	450-500Fo	232-260Co	7-8-9-10	" "

Spices you must have at home
Parsley (for garnish different foods)
Mint
Rosemary
Laurel
Thyme
Dried Garlic
Red pepper dry or fresh
Celery
Dried basil
Oregano
Cumin
Walnut
Pabrika
Pepper in powder and corns, black and white
Cinnamon ground and whole
Nutmeg
Cloves
Pickle caper
Dinenuts

FOREWORD

Every man, since he was born and during his life, his main care is choosing and eating healthy foods.

To succeed at this attempt choosing the cor rect food is not enough. He needes to know the way to prepar the food.

In this book you will find the ways to make genuine Greek foods and cakes, so every one who will attempt to cook according to them, will have a satisfactory if not, an excellent result.

Greek cuisine has a great variety of foods and cakes, and is considered one of the bests cusines of the world.

In this book you will find representative recipes from all Greek areas. Before the writer decided to share her knowledge, she went around Greece, asked, learned and most importantly she cooked their foods, and gave pleasure and gastro nomical enjoyment to many friends.

Of course it is not forbiden for any woman, who decides to cook a recipe from this book, to take some initiatives and change any recipe in order to suit the tastes and the preferances of her guests.

For example: To add more or not at all, salt, pepper, oil, vinegar, or even increase or reduce the portions. We believe that with the edition of this book we present the possibility for every woman to smile with satisfaction and gladness every time which after an enjoyable meal, she listens to her friends ask her the recipe, so they can cook it too.

Good appetite
The publisher.

APPETIZERS

APPETIZER WITH CRAB

OREKTIKO ME KAVOURI

Preparation time 30 minutes   For 5 persons

400gr. caned of crab (1 lb, or 14 OZ)
100gr. crumble cheese (1/4 lb, or 4 OZ)
200gr. beaten milk cream (1/2 lb, or 7 OZ)
100gr. Butter (1/4 lb, or 4 OZ)
1 Table spoon lemon juice
1 Small glass cognac (1/4 lb, or 4 OZ)
salt if you prefer
Pepper if you prefer

PASTRY WITH ROQUEFORT CHEESE

PITAKIA ME ROKFOR

Preparation time 30 minutes   20 pieces

1 portion pastry sheets for cheese pasties see piecrust or pastry sheets (p
250gr. Roquefort cheese (1/2 lb, or 9 OZ)
1 egg beaten
150gr. Butter (1/4 lb, or 5 OZ)

CHEESE FOR OUZO

TIRAKIA GIA OUZO

Preparation time 30 minutes   30 pieces

100gr. Butter (1/4 lb, or 4 OZ)
4 eggs
100gr. grated cheese (1/4 lb, or 4 OZ)
150gr. Flour (1/4 lb, or 5 OZ)
200gr. water (1/2 lb, or 7 OZ)
nutmeg, salt, and pepper.

Strain crab meat of its water for few minutes. Put in a mixer the butter, pepper, cheese and crab, and melt them, to make a thick mass.

Add the lemon, the salt, and the cognac and mix very well. Put the milk cream, and mix very well, to make all a mixture.

Put it in a platter and refrigerate
3 to 4 hours, before serving.

Serve with cabbage salad or lettuce salad.

Prepare the pastry sheet (phyllo) for cheese pies.

It must be one inch thick.

Melt the butter and mix it with the roquefort cheese.

Cut the pastry sheet (phyllo) into medium pieces, square trianglar, or round.

Over each piece put a teaspoon of the mixture.

Wet the tips of pastry and cover it with another piece of phyllo.

Press with a fork to stack the tips and brush with a beaten egg.

Butter a pan, put them in, and bake in a very warm oven for 15 minutes.

You can serve them cold or hot.

In a saucepan, put the water, the butter and the flour, and bring to a boil. Mix continuously with a wooden spoon.

When the paste, starts to separate from the sides of the saucepan, remove from heat. Add eggs one by one, mix well, until the eggs are completely mixed. Add the cheese, nutmeg, salt and pepper stirring continuously, until it will become a uniform mixture.

Heat three cups olive oil in a frying pan and with a table spoon drop paste in the pan. After a few minutes   when they are golden brown they are ready. Drain them. You can serve them hot or cold.

BOILED SNAILS

SALIGARIA VRASTA

Preparation time 120 minutes

1 kilo trade snails small (2 lb, or 36 OZ)
1 Lemon
Salt

The trade snails are dry and torpid, so you can use them at once.
Put the snails in water, one hour before you will use them.
With a pointed knife, clean them around the mouth of the shell.
Pinch them and if they move they are alive.
Wash them many times.
Put them in a saucepan, cover them with water, add some salt and boil for 15 minutes.
During the boiling remove the foam.
Drain them, add the lemon and serve.

FRIED SNAILS

SALIGARIA TIGANITA

Preparation time 90 minutes

1 kilo trade snails big (2 lb, or 36 OZ)
100gr. (1/4 lb or 4 OZ) vinegar or red wine
salt

With a pointed knife, clean the snails, around the mouth of the shell. Pinch them and if they move, they are alive.
Wash them many times and live them for 25 minutes to drain.
Take snails one by one and put some salt in the mouth of the shell. They will start to put out a kind of yellow liquid.
Heat two cups olive oil and put the snails one by one in the frying pan, with the mouth down to the pan. Fry them for 5 minutes, add the vinegar or the wine, cook for 2 minutes. Remove from the heat and serve immediately.

BOILED OCTOPUS

HTAPODI VRASTO

Preparation time 2 hours

2 small octopus
3/4 of cup olive oil
1/4 of cup vinegar or lemon
salt and pepper

BOILED SHRIMPS

GARIDES VRASTES

Preparation time 1 hour

1 kilo shrimps (2 lb, or 36 OZ)
1/2 cup vinegar
3/4 of cup olive oil
1/4 of cup lemon juice

CODFISH CROQUETTES

KROKETES BAKALIAROU

Preparation time 1 hour

3 cups codfish dried
5 cups potatoes
3 table spoons butter
4 eggs
3 tablespoons onion chopped
3 tablespoons parsley chopped
salt and white pepper

Wash the octopus very good. Put them into a pan, cover them with water, add salt, and boil for 1 1/2 hour.

When they become soft (piece with a fork) drain and cool. Peel off the skin, and cut them in small pieces.

Pour over the octopus the olive oil and the vinegar.

Serve cold.

Wash the shrimps. Put them in a saucepan, cover them with water, add the vinegar, and boil for 25 minutes.

Drain, remove their shell and put them in a platter.

Pour over them the olive oil and the lemon.

Serve cold.

Soak the codfish in water for 24 hours. Boil it for 15 minutes. Let it cool, remove the skin and the bones. Cut in very small pieces, and measure 3 cups godfish meat.

Boiled the potatoes and mash them.

Mix them with the codfish, eggs, onion, butter, parsley, salt and pepper.

Mix very well until it is a uniform mixture.

Shape with your hands into croquettes, round or oblong.

Fry them in very hot olive oil on low heat until golden brown.

Drain on paper towels to remove excess oil and serve hot.

FRIED MEAT BALLS

KEFTEDAKIA

Preparation time 45 minutes   For 10 persons@T3 =

1 kilo ground meat veal or beef (2 lb, or 36 OZ)
1 1/2 cup bread crumbs
1 large onion
1 tea spoon mint
1 tablespoon lemon juice
1 tablespoon olive oil
1 tablespoon parsley
salt and pepper
1 tea spoon oregano
3 cups olive oil for frying

Put the ground meat in a bowl. Add the oregano, bread, parsley, mint, lemon, 1 tablespoon olive oil, salt and pepper, and the onion cut in very small pieces. Mix them all together very well. Make small balls. Fry them in a pan with the 3 cups olive oil, until browned all sides. Serve hot or cold.

FRIED SQUID

KALAMARAKIA TIGANITA

Preparation time 50 minutes   For 6 persons

1 kilo squids (2 lb, or 36 OZ)
1/2 kilo olive oil (1 lb, or 18 OZ)
1 lemon
Flour and salt

Wash the squids very good. Cut the tresses and remove the ink sacks. Remove the eyes and the fine bone. Remove the skin from the hoods and cut them into round pieces. Wash them very good and drain them. Add the salt. Flour them lightly. Put the olive oil in a frying pan and heat it until hot. Fry the squids until they turn light brown. Pour the lemon juice over them and serve hot.

CHEESE PASTIES

TIROPITAKIA

Preparation time 50 minutes   50 pieces

1/2 kilo Feta cheese (1 lb, or 18 OZ)
4 eggs
1 cup milk
20 phyllo leaves
5 tablespoons Flour
4 tablespoons butter
salt, pepper, butter for the leaves

Bring milk to a boil. Put the butter in a saucepan and melt it. Add the flour and mix very well. Add the milk, salt and pepper. Mix them to make a jelly cream.

Remove from heat and let cool.

Cut the cheese in very small pieces. Beat the eggs. Put the cheese pieces and the eggs in the cream. Mix very well.

Cut the phyllo leaves as broadly as you want.

Brush each phyllo leaf with butter. Put at the biginning of phyllo, with a teaspoon, some stuffing.

Fold back the phyllo ends, over the stuffing. Fold in triagular form.

Butter them. Butter a baking pan, and lay them in.

Bake them in a medium oven for 20 minutes until they turn light brown.

Serve them hot.
Note: You can fry them in a low fire, until golden brown.

MINCED MEAT FILLED ROLLS

BOUREKAKIA APO KIMA

Preparation time 1 hour 40 pieces

1/2 kilo minced meat (1 lb, or 18 OZ)
1 small can tomato peelings
1/2 cup chopped cheese
1 chopped onion
1 cup butter
20 phyllo leaves ready made
1 table spoon chopped parsley
1/2 tea spoon cinnamon dust
salt and pepper

STUFFED GRAPEVINE LEAVES

DOLMADAKIA ME RIZI

Preparation time 1 1/2 hour 30 pieces

30 fresh grapevine leaves
3 chopped onions
250 gr. olive oil (1/2 lb, or 9 OZ)
1 cup olive oil
250gr. rice (1/2 lb, or 9 OZ)
2 table spoon fresh dill chopped
2 table spoon chopped parsley
1 tea spoon cumin
2 lemons
1/2 tea spoon chooped mint
1 cup water
salt and pepper

In a saucepan, put the minced meat with the half butter and the chopped onion and saute for 10 minutes.

Chopp the tomatoes in the mixer and add them with the salt, pepper, parsley and cinnamon in the minced meat.

Cook in a low fire for half an hour.

Remove from the fire and add the cheese and mix them well.

Cut the phyllo leaves as broadly as you want.

Brush each phyllo leaf, with butter. Put at the bigining of phyllo, a table spoon of stuffing. Fold back the phyllo ends on the stuffing and roll them up. Butter them.

Butter a baking pan and lay them in. Bake them in moderate oven for 20 minutes, until tern light brown, or fry them.

Serve them hot.

Wash the grapevine leaves very well and cut off, their stalk. Put them in a saucepan, cover them with water and boil them for 5 minutes. Strain and rinse them in cold water.

Put in a bowl the rice, onion dill, parsley, cumin, mint, salt, pepper, 250gr. olive oil, and the lemon juice. Mix them very well to make a mixture.

Take each leaf from the wrong side, and put on it 1 tea spoon of stuffing. Fold the ends of the leaf on the stuffing and roll it up.

Put them in a shallow saucepan covering the bottom with the vine leaves. After you will finish the bottom, continue puting vine leaves on top of the others, until finish. Add in them the 1 cup olive oil and water, to cover them. Put over the vine leaves a plate to protect them from unwrapping, during cooking. Cook them about 1 hour on a low fire.

Serve them cold with yogourt or warm.

SALADS

MEAT SALAD

KREATOSALATA

Preparation time 15 minutes   For 4 persons

1 1/2 cup chopped left over and boiled meat
1 cup cucumber chopped
1 1/2 cup chopped and boiled potatoes
1 cup chopped and boiled beet-roots
2 cups mayonnaise
2 table spoons chopped onion
2 table spoons chopped parsley
White pepper and salt

Use left over meat.
Mix in a bowl, all the ingredients and half of the mayonnaise. The remaining mayonnaise put it over the mixture like cream.
Eat the salad immediately.

POTATO SALAD

PATATOSALATA

Preparation time 30 minutes   For 6 persons

1 kilo potatoes (2 lb, or 36 OZ)
1/2 cup vinegar
1 cup olive oil
3 hard boiled eggs chopped
3 table spoons chopped parsley
1 chopped onion
salt and pepper

Skin the potatoes, cut into small pieces and wash. Cover the potatoes with salty water, and boil for 20 minutes.
Drain and put in a bowl. In an other bowl, mix the vinegar, olive oil, eggs, parsley, onion, salt and pepper. Mix very well.
Pour this sauce over the potatoes, mix well and serve.
Note: You may also use mayonnaise. Use about 1 cup.

CHICKEN SALAD

SALATA ME KOTOPOULO

Preparation time 20 minutes   For 6 persons

2 cups chopped boiled chicken
1 table spoon onion juice
1 table spoon chopped parsley
1/2 cup ketchup
1/2 cup mayonnaise

SHRIMP SALAD

GARIDOSALATA

Preparation time 50 minutes   For 6 persons

1 kilo shrimps (2 lb, or 36 OZ)
3 hard boiled eggs chopped
1 portion mayonnaise (see mayonnaise sauce)
1 table spoon caper
salt and pepper

VILLAGE SALAD

SALATA HORIATIKI

Preparation time 15 minutes   For 6 persons

2 large Tomatoes
2 cucumber medium size
1 onion
2 green bell-pepper
2 hard boiled eggs
10 olives
3 table spoons olive oil
1 tea spoon vinegar
150gr. feta cheese, salt

Mix in a bowl all the ingredients very well to make a uniform mixture.

Chill in the refrigerator for 1 hour and serve.

Wash and boil the shrimps for 20 minutes. Drain and take off their shell. Put them in a bowl. Add eggs, caper, mayonnaise, salt and pepper and mix well. Serve cold.

Wash the vegetables and cut them in pieces. Put them in a bowl. Pour them, with the olive oil, the salt and the vinegar. Add the olives and feta cheese. Mix well and serve.

ARTICHOKE SALAD

AGINARES SALATA

Preparation time 40 minutes   For 6 persons

12 medium artichokes
2 lemons
1/2 cup olive oil
salt and pepper

LETTUCE SALAD

MAROULOSALATA

Preparation time 15 minutes   For 4 persons

2 medium heads of lettuce
2 fresh scallions
5 pieces of dill fresh stalks
1/2 cup olive oil
1/4 of cup vinegar, salt

CABBAGE AND CARROT SALAD

LAHANO KE KAROTA SALATA

Preparation time 15 minutes   For 4 persons

1 kilo solid cabbage white or red (2 lb, or 36 OZ)
2 medium carrots grated
3/4 of cup olive oil
1/4 of cup vinegar, salt

Remove the outer leaves of the artichokes, pulling them one by one. Cut the artichokes in two parts. Emptying them of their fluff. Rub artichokes with lemon, so they will not blacken, and drop them in water, with lemon juice in, until finish with all of the artichokes.

Mix the olive oil and the lemon very well.

Drain the artichokes and pour them with the oil and lemon. Add some salt and pepper and serve, in four pieces each one person.

Wash the lettuce leaf by leaf and let them drain. Take 4-5 leaves and cut them in thin pieces.

Continue like that until finished with leaves.

In the same way cut scallions and dill.

Put them in a bowl all together and add the olive oil, vinegar and salt. Mix them very well, and serve.

Remove the outer leaves of the cabbage and cut it into two parts. Take the one part and cut it in thin strips. Do the same with the second half.

Grate carrots. Wash the cabbage very well and drain. Put it in a bowl with the grated carrots, add the olive oil, vinegar, and salt.

Mix them all together and serve.

CUCUMBER GARLIC AND YOGHOURT SALAD

TZATZIKI

Preparation time 30 minutes   For 8 persons

1 large cucumber grated
4 cloves garlic
1/2 kilo yoghourt (1 lb, or 18 OZ)
3 table spoons olive oil
1 table spoon vinegar
salt and pepper

Do not peel the cucumber. Wash it only, grate and leave it for 5 minutes to drain. Crush the garlic.

In a bowl, put the yoghourt, cucumber, garlic, vinegar, salt and pepper. Mix them together adding the olive oil little by little, mixing continuously.

Refrigerate for 1 hour and serve.

BOILED CAULIFLOWER SALAD

KOUNOUPIDI VRASTO SALATA

Preparation time 30 minutes   For 4 persons

2 kilos cauliflower (4 lb, or 72 OZ)
1 cup olive oil
2 lemons, salt

Cut off the stem of the cauliflower and the outer green leaves. Cut it in four pieces, check it for worms, and wash it very good.

Put it in a pan of salted water and bring to a boil. When the water start boiling put the cauliflower in, and boil it on high heat for half an hour.

(The stalk pieces of the cauliflower, must be at the bottom of the pan).

Drain it and put it in a bowl. Let it cool.

Serve it with the olive oil and lemon.

TOMATO AND CUCUMBER SALAD

AGOUROTOMATOSALATA

Preparation time 10 minutes   For 2 persons

2 medium tomatoes
2 cucumbers medium size
3/4 of cup olive oil
2 table spoons vinegar, salt

EGGPLANT SALAD

MELITZANOSALATA

Preparation time 50 minutes   For 4 persons

1/2 kilo egg plants (1 lb, or 18 OZ)
1 fresh onion
1 green bell pepper
200gr. mayonnaise (1/2 lb, or 7 OZ)

EGGS

MEDIUM BOILED EGGS

AVGA VRASTA MELATA

BAKED EGGS WITH SPINACH

AVGA ME SPANAKI STO FOURNO

Preparation time 55 minutes   For 5 persons

1/2 kilo fresh spinach or canned (1 lb, or 18 OZ)
5 eggs
200gr. parmezana cheese (1/2 lb, or 7 OZ)
3 table spoons butter
salt and pepper

Wash the tomatoes. Peel cucumbers. Cut them in pieces. Put them in a bowl and add the olive oil, vinegar, salt and serve.

NOTE: You can add cabbage, or lettuce, or green peppers if you want.

Wash the egg plants. Pierce them with a fork and soften them by pressing them with your hands. Bake them in a moderate oven about half an hour. Remove their peel and the seeds.

Mash them.

In a bowl chopped the onion and the bell pepper.

Add the egg plants, mayonnaise and mix well.

Serve cold.

Put the eggs in water and boil them for 2 minutes. Take them out of the water and rinse them in cold water for 2 minutes. Serve.

Bring the salted water to a boil and put the spinach in, to boil. Drain spinach and put it in a baking pan. Melt the butter and pour over the spinach. Grate cheese and pour over the spinach. Make holes in spinach just large enough for the eggs to be placed in them. Break the eggs and put them in these holes.

Bake them in warm oven for 15 minutes, until the eggs are cooked. Serve warm.

SHRIMP OMELETTE

OMELETA ME GARIDES

Preparation time 30 minutes   For 4 persons

6 eggs
7 table spoons butter
1 table spoon butter
5 table spoons milk
1 cup boiled shrimps, chopped
salt and pepper

Boil the shrimps and take off their shells. Put them in a frying pan with the 1 table spoon of the butter and cook for 2 minutes. Beat the eggs and put salt and pepper. Mix them with the milk. In another frying pan, melt the 7 table spoons butter. Add the shrimps and the eggs together. Fry them over low heat on both sides.

Cut the omelette in four pieces and serve one piece to each person.

MUSHROOM OMELETTE

OMELETA ME MANITARIA

Preparation time 20 minutes   For 6 persons

1 medium canned of mushrooms
8 eggs
4 table spoons milk
8 table spoons butter
1 table spoon butter (for the mushrooms)
salt and pepper

Drain the mushrooms of their liquid and cut them in pieces. Melt the 1 table spoon butter and put the mushrooms in pan and cook for 2 minutes. Beat the eggs, add the milk, salt and pepper. In a frying pan, put the 8 table spoons butter to melt. Add the eggs and the mushrooms. Fry them over low heat turning to cook both sides.

Cut in six pieces and served hot.

EGGS STUFFED

AVGA GEMISTA

Preparation time 20 minutes   For 4 persons

8 hard boiled eggs
3 table spoons butter
1 cup canned chopped crab meat
1 tea spoon mustard
1 table spoon chopped parsley
1 table spoon pickle chopped
1 tea spoon capers
salt and pepper

FRIED EGGS IN TOMATO SAUCE

AVGA ME TOMATES

Preparation time 30 minutes   For 6 persons

3/4 of kilo red tomatoes (1 3/4 lb, or 28 OZ)
6 eggs
1 cup olive oil
salt and pepper

EGGS ROLLED UP WITH GROUND MEAT

AVGA TYLIGMENA ME KIMA

Preparation time 60 minutes   For 4 persons

8 hard boiled eggs
750gr. ground meat (1 3/4 lb, or 28 OZ)
2 toast bread crumbs for the ground meat
1/2 cup toast bread crumbs
1/2 kilo red tomatoes (1 lb, or 18 OZ)
1 table spoon chopped parsley
1 egg
1 tea spoon cinnamon
3 cups olive oil for frying
salt and pepper

Boil the eggs for 10 minutes. Peel the eggs, without touching the white of the eggs. Cut them in two parts. Take out the yolk. Cut under the white, a piece so the eggs can stand on the plate.

Mix the yolks with the butter until smooth and creamy. Add the crabs, mustard, cucumber, salt and pepper. Mix them all together well.

Fill the white of the eggs with a tea spoonful of yolk mixture.

Sprinkle some parsley and place one piece of caper on top. Serve them on buttery crackers, 4 pieces of egg to each person.

Wash the tomatoes very good. Grind them to be a pulpy. Heat the olive oil and add the tomatoes pulp. Cook for 20 minutes. Put the eggs, one by one equally spaced in the tomato sauce. Season with salt. With a table spoon take some sauce and pour on the top of the egg until they are cooked.

Serve hot, one egg to each person.

Put the ground meat in a bowl and make a hole in the middle. Put in the 2 toast bread crumbs, the yolk of 1 egg, parsley, salt and pepper. Mix well. Boil the 8 eggs until well cooked. Peel them, without touching the white.

Make 8 balls with the ground meat.

Take each ball mold it with your fingers and put each egg into it. Cover with the ground meat molded well so it will not break during frying.

Roll each ball in the toast bread crumbs.

Heat the olive oil in a fry pan until hot and then lower the flame. Put the balls in the pan and fry them.

After you finish frying, ground the tomatoes to be a pulp. Add them in the same olive oil in which you fried the ground meat balls. Add the cinnamon and let the sauce coagulate.

Cut each ball in two parts and put them in the sauce for 10 minutes. Served hot with fried potatoes, or mashed potatoes.

SAUCES

BECHAMEL SAUCE REGULAR

SALTSA BESSAMEL KANONIKI

1 portion for medium pan

6 table spoons butter
4 cups milk
8 table spoons flour
2 egg yolks beaten well
salt and white pepper

GREEN SAUCE

PRASINI SALTSA

2 cups mayonnaise
2 bunches of parsley (fresh)

MAYONNAISE SAUCE EASY AND QUICK

MAYONEZA EFKOLI TIS STIGMIS

2 egg yolks
8 table spoons corn flour
1 cup water
2 tea spoons dry mustard
1 cup milk
2 tea spoons vinegar
1 tea spoon salt
1/2 tea spoon white pepper
3 table spoons lemon juice
1/2 cup olive oil

40

Bring milk to a boil. Put the butter in a saucepan to melt. Add the flour little by little and mix continuosly until creamy.

Remove the sauce pan from the fire and add the milk little by little mixing continuosly. Put on the fire again, and mix well to make the sauce smooth and creamy. Remove from fire, add the salt, pepper, 2 beaten yolks and mix very well.

Note: If will not use the sauce immediately, mix it, so it will not form a crust on top, occasionally.

Wash the parsley and chopped its leaves, and mince. Take a table spoon of the parsley's juice and add it to the mayonnaise. Mix very well.

The sauce will become a green colour.

Served mostly with sea food.

Dissolve the corn flour in the half water. Mix other half water with the milk and bring to a boil. Add the corn flour, mixing continuosly until it will be like cream.

Put it in a bowl and let it cool.

In an other bowl put the mustard, vinegar, yolks, pepper, salt and mix them together.

Add them little by little in the cream, mixing continuosly add little olive oil and little lemon juice until they are well mixed.

Mix the mayonnaise very well and put it in the refrigerator.

Use sauce when you want.

BRAINS SAUCE

SALTSA ME MIALA

1 cup boiled brains
2 cups mayonnaise sauce
2 table spoons chopped parsley
salt and pepper

MUSTARD SAUCE

SALTSA MOUSTARDAS

3 table spoons butter
3 table spoons flour
1 1/2 table spoon dry mustard
1 cup boiled meat broth or beef bouillon cube
salt and pepper

TUNA SAUCE

SATLSA TONOU

1 cup olive oil
1/2 kilo red tomatoes (1 lb, or 18 OZ)
1/2 cup grated cheese
1/2 cup canned tuna
2 table spoons chopped parsley
2 bay leaves
2 cloves garlic, salt, pepper

WHITE MUSHROOM SAUCE

SALTSA LEFKI MANITARION

1 medium can of mushrooms
1 cup milk
1 cup grated cheese
1/2 cup milk cream
2 table spoons butter
2 table spoons flour
2 egg yolks, salt and pepper

Put the brains in tepid water for 1 hour so the blood comes out and the membrane will soften.

Drain them and very carefully remove the membranes.

Put brains in a sauce pan and cover them with water. Add some salt and some vinegar, and boil for 15 minutes.

Drain let them cool, and cook as you like.

Now, **for the sauce:**

After boil the brains, cut them in small pieces, and mix in mayonnaise. Add the parsley, salt, pepper, and mix well to make a uniform creamy sauce.

Melt the butter and mix flour in it until dissolved. Add immediately the meat juice and mix until the sauce thickens.

Remove from the fire, add the mustard, salt and pepper.

Let it cool and serve, with boiled fish.

You can use the juice from boiled fish, also.

Clean and cut the garlic into very small pieces. Chopp the tuna and mix it with the parsley. Grind the tomatoes. Put them with the olive oil to brown, add the garlic, bay leaves, salt and pepper, and cook until sauce thickens. Add the tuna with the parsley and cook for 10 minutes.

Remove from the fire and mix the sauce with the cheese very well. This is a very tasty sauce for macaroni or fried potatoes.

Melt the butter and mix well with the flour. Heat the milk adding the butter to make a cream. Remove from the fire, let it cool, add the yolks, cheese, and mix very well. Add the mushrooms, the milk cream, salt and pepper. Served with boiled meats.

SAUCE FOR ROASTED MEAT

SALTSA PSITOU

4 table spoons butter
2 cups water
3 table spoons flour
salt and pepper
2 cups of the roast meat juice

Put in a saucepan the butter and melt it. Heat, add the salt and pepper, flour and mix them very well. Let it lightly brown. Heat the water in which you will mix the juice of the roast meat. Add it in the saucepan and boil all together for 5 minutes.

Serve the sauce hot.

VERY - VERY HOT SAUCE

SALTSA POLI KAFTERI

2 large onions grated pulpifyed
1 table spoon mustard
2 cups white wine
3 table spoons ketchup
1 bouillon cube
salt and pepper

Put the wine in a saucepan. Add the onion pulp, the bouillon cube and boil them for 20 minutes. Remove from the fire, add the mustard, ketchup, salt and pepper. Mix very well.

Served mostly with poultry or with grilled meat.

OLIVE OIL AND LEMON SAUCE

SALTSA LADOLEMONO

1 cup olive oil
2 large lemons

Beat the olive oil with the lemon juice very good to mix all together.

Serve with salads, or fish, or grilled meats.

SAUCE FOR GRILL MEAT

SALTSA GIA PSITA SHARAS

1 large chopped onion
8 table spoons olive oil
2 cloves garlic (chopped)
1 tea spoon mustard
1 tea spoon vinegar
1 tea spoon powder thyme
1 tea spoon sugar
1 small glass white wine (100gr, or 1/4 lb, or 4 OZ)
3 table spoons tomato juice, salt and pepper

Put in a saucepan olive oil and the onion to saute. Add the wine, tomato juice, vinegar and let them boil for 10 minutes. Add the chopped garlic, sugar, thyme, mustard, salt and pepper and cook for 40 minutes on low fire. Mash and serve. You can serve with all grilled meats.

GARLIC SAUCE

SKORDALIA

6 cloves of garlic crushed
2 cups mashed and boiled potatoes (500gr. or 1 lb, or 18 OZ)
1 cup olive oil, 1/4 of cup vinegar.

Peel wash, cut the potatoes, and boil them in salted water until cooked. Drain and mash them. In a bowl put the potatoes, crushed garlic, olive oil and the vinegar little by little, until they finish, and mix well all the time. When the sauce starts to hold its shape, stop mixing. Serve cold with fried fish, eegplant or squash.

EGG AND LEMON SAUCE

AVGOLEMONO

3 eggs
1 large lemon

OLIVE OIL AND TOMATO SAUCE

SALTSA DOMATA ME LADI

1 kilo red tomatoes (2 lb, or 36 OZ)
250gr. (1/2 lb, or 9 OZ) olive oil
1 large onion, chopped
3 cloves garlic
2 bay leaves
1 large carrot
3 table spoons chopped parsley
3 table spoons flour
1 tea spoon sugar
salt and red pepper

EASY DISHES

POTATO BALLS

PATATOKEFTEDES

Preparation time 40 minutes For 8 persons

1 kilo (2 lb, or 36 OZ) potatoes
5 egg yolks
4 table spoons butter
4 table spoons toast crumbs
1 teaspoon crushed nutmeg
2 cups olive oil for frying
Flour for coating
Salt and white pepper

Keep a cup broth of the soup you are making. Beat the eggs very good. Add lemon juice and beat continuously. Add the broth little by little until it will finish.

Remove the soup from the fire. Add the sauce to it and mix all together very good.

This sauce is served mostly with meat soup, or fish soup, or meat balls soup.

Put the olive oil in a saucepan and add the onion, garlic, bay leaves, carrot cut in two pieces and the parsley. Cook all together for 10 minutes with a low fire. Add the flour, mixing continuously. When they are all light brown, chop the tomatoes, and put them in the saucepan, with the salt, pepper, sugar, and a little water.

Cook them all, for half an hour.

Remove from fire and grind them. The sauce is ready.

Serve with macaroni, or meat, or cooked rice.

Peel and boil the potatoes. Drain and grind them. Add the butter, toast crumbs, nutmeg, salt, pepper and eggs.

Mold them in small balls the size of a walnut.

Lightly flour the balls and fry them in olive oil.

Serve hot.

SOUVLAKIA WITH SAUSAGES

SOUVLAKIA ME LOUKANIKA

Preparation time 45 minutes For 6 persons

6 sausages links
5 squash
10 small onions
200gr. (7 OZ, or 1/2 lb) butter
salt and pepper

BAKED POTATOES

PATATES FOURNOU

Preparation time 60 minutes For 5 persons

1 kilo (36 OZ, or 2 lb) small potatoes
2 bouillon cubes
600gr. (21 OZ, or 1 1/4 lb) water
100gr. (4 OZ, or 1/4 lb) butter
2-3 cloves garlic
Juice of 1 lemon
salt and pepper

FRIED SQUASH

KOLOKITHAKIA TIGANITA

Preparation time 30 minutes   For 5 persons

1 kilo (2 lb, or 36 OZ) squash
500gr. (1 lb, or 18 OZ) olive oil for frying
salt and pepper, flour

FRESH BEANS WITH BUTTER

FASOLAKIA FRESKA ME VOUTYRO

Preparation time 30 minutes For 4 persons

1 kilo (36 OZ, or 2 lb) fresh beans
300gr. (10 OZ, or 3/4 lb) water
1 cube bouillon
100gr. (4 OZ, or 1/4 lb) margarine, salt.

48

Boil the squash and the onions in salted water, until they become soft. Drain, cut the squash, in 4 pieces each, and the sausages in 4 pieces too. Put all the pieces in skewers like this: sausage, squash, onion (whole), sausage, until all the pieces are used. Start always with sausage and finsih with sausage. Salt them. Then fry them in the butter.

Serve hot with cabbage salad, or pilaf or fried potatoes.

Pell, wash and cut the potatoes in thick slices. Put them in a baking pan. Boil the water with the cubes until dissolved. Add the lemon, garlic, and add them to the baking pan. Add the butter, salt and pepper and put them in a hot oven for 1 hour until baked.

Serve with meat or poultry, baked or grilled.

Clean and wash the squash. Do not peel. Cut them lengthwise and let them drain. Heat the olive oil. Put salt and pepper on the squash. Coat squash with flour and fry them until golden brown. Drain them on paper towels and serve hot.

Clean the fibrils from the beans. Wash them and boil in salty water in which you have dissolved the bouillon cube, for 20 minutes. Drain, add the melted margarine and saute them for 10 minutes.

Serve with meat or chicken, roasted or grilled.

SMALL CHEESE PIES

MIKRES PITES ME TYRI

Preparation time 30 minutes For 4 persons

4 small pieces of feta cheese
3 egg yolks and 1 egg white beaten
4 table spoons flour
4 table spoons grated cheese for macaroni
250gr. (1/2 lb, or 9 OZ) olive oil for frying
1 medium onion (chopped)
salt and pepper

CHEESE ROLLS

ROLA ME TYRI

Preparation time 40 minutes For 6 persons

200gr. (1/2 lb, or 7 OZ) boiled chicken in small pieces
5 table spoons chopped cheese
6 big slices of ham
1 cup wet bread in milk
4 table spoons wine
100gr. (1/4 lb, or 3 OZ) butter
100gr. cheese you prefare, cut in thin slices
2 eggs
3 table spoons flour
salt and pepper

SOUPS

VEGETABLE SOUP

HORTOSOUPA

Preparation time 1 1/2 hour   For 4 persons

4 table spoons olive oil
3 onions
1 stalk of celery
1/2 kilo (18 oz, or 1 lb) potatoes
5 carrots
1/2 kilo (18 OZ, or 1 lb) red tomatoes or 1 big can@T2 =
salt and pepper

Beat the yolks. Add the onion, feta cheese, grated cheese, beaten egg white, flour, salt and pepper. Mix well to make a uniform mixture. Take some mixture and mold with your hands, making pies in the shape you prefer. Fry them in very hot olive oil, until golden brown.
Serve hot or cold.

Mush the chicken with the bread. Put them in a bowl. Add the 5 table spoons cheese, eggs, salt, pepper and the flour. Mix them all together very well. Fill the slices of ham with this mixture. Roll them, and pin them with a toothpick in the middle, so they will not unwrap.

Melt the butter in a saucepan and fry them for 5 minutes. Add the wine and place a slice of the cheese you prefer on top of each.

Cook them with a low flame for 10 minutes. When the cheese starts to melt, remove from flame and serve immediately.

Clean, wash and cut in small pieces all the vegetables. Boil them for 20 minutes, then add the tomatoes cut in small pieces, salt and continue boiling for half an hour. Remove from the fire and grind them. Put the pulp in the saucepan, add melted butter, pepper and mix all together. Serve hot.

SPINACH SOUP

SOUPA ME SPANAKI

Preparation time 1 hour For 4 persons

1/2 kilo (18 OZ, or 1 lb)spinach
6 cups water or any meat broth
2 table spoons butter
4 table spoons rice flour
3 table spoons chopped cheese, salt and pepper

CABBAGE SOUP

SOUPA ME LAHANO

Preparation time 1 1/2 hour For 8 persons

2 cups chopped cabbage
1 cup chopped onion
1/2 cup butter
13 cups water
1 cup chopped sausage
1/2 table spoon chopped dill, salt and pepper

BEAN SOUP

SOUPA FASOLIA

Preparation time 60 minutes For 6 persons

3 cups dried beans
1/2 kilo (1 lb, or 18 OZ) ripe tomatoes
3 stalks of celery
1 large chopped onion, 2 carrots
1 cup olive oil, salt and pepper

Clean, wash and cut spinach in small pieces. Drain. Boil it in water until cooked. Drain. Melt the butter in a saucepan, add the spinach and saute. In an other saucepan put the riceflour, spinach and thin little by little, with the very hot broth. Boil them for 15 minutes in low fire mixing all the time, add cheese, boil 5 more minutes remove from the fire. Serve hot.

Put the chopped cabbage in boiling water and boil for 5 to 7 minutes. Drain. In a saucepan melt the butter add the chopped onion to light brown. Add the water and let them boil. Add the cabbage, sausage, dill, salt and pepper and cook together for 1 hour, until the cabbage and onions are soft. Serve hot.

Wash the beans and soak them over night. Next day rinse them, put in a saucepan and cover with water. Boil for 45 minutes. Drain and reserve the water. In the same saucepan add the onion, the ground tomatoes, olive oil, celery, carrots and lightly brown. Add the beans, salt and pepper and after 5 minutes add the water you have reserved. Boil for 10 minutes longer. Serve hot.

CHICK-PEA SOUP

SOUPA REVITHIA

Preparation time 90 minutes For 5 persons

500gr. (1 lb, or 18 OZ) peeled chick-peas
2 table spoons baking soda
1 cup olive oil
2 chopped onions
2 table spoons flour
The juice from 2 lemons, salt and pepper

BEER SOUP

SOUPA ME BIRA

Preparation time 30 minutes For 5 persons

4 table spoons flour
3 table spoons butter
(1/2 lb, or 18 OZ) beer
4 table spoons grated cheese
(1/2 lb, or 18 OZ) meat broth
(250gr. 9 OZ, or 1/2 lb) milk
1 tea spoon sugar
1 tea spoon cinnamon powder, salt and pepper

LENTIL SOUP

FAKES SOUPA

Preparation time 60 minutes For 6 persons

3 cups lentils
1 large chopped onion
1 cup olive oil
2 bay leaves
10 cloves of garlic
1/2 kilo (1 lb, or 18 OZ) ripe tomatoes or 1 can tomatoes
salt and pepper

Put the chick peas in water to soak, over night.

Next morning, drain them, and mix them with the baking soda for 15 minutes. Wash off with hot water very well. Put them in a saucepan and cover them with water. Boil them for half an hour to 45 minutes. Taking off the foam. When chick peas will start to dissolve, add the olive oil, onion, salt and pepper and boil for 10 minutes.

Dissolve the flour in the lemon juice, adding some juice from the chick peas. Add it little by little, mixing very well. Add this mixture to the boiling chick peas and let them boil for 5 more minutes. Remove from the fire and serve hot.

Put the butter in a saucepan and melt. Add the flour and cook until brown. Mix continuously and add little beer and meat broth. Add the cinnamon, salt, pepper and sugar. Boil over low fire for 20 minutes. Add milk and, mix well removing from the fire. Serve hot, with the grated cheese over the soup.

Wash the lentils and boil with water for 45 minutes. Drain the water reserving it. (Because in that water, are all the lentil's vitamins). In the same saucepan put the olive oil, onion ground tomatoes, garlic and bay leaves. Cook them until lightly brown. Add the lentils, salt and pepper and as soon as it boils, add the water from the lentils you have reserved. Let them boil approximately 20 minutes. Serve hot.

EASTER SOUP

MAYIRITSA

Preparation time 90 minutes For 6 persons

The liver, heart and the intestines of a lamb
1 chopped onion
2 table spoons dill
4 table spoons butter
2 table spoons fresh onions chopped
3 eggs
Meat broth in proportion to amount of rice (here 7 cups)
6 table spoons rice, salt and pepper
juice of 2 lemons

    Clean the meat and scald it in boiling water. Let it cool and cut it in small pieces. In a saucepan, melt the butter. Add the onion to lightly brown, meat, fresh onions, dill, salt and pepper and the meat broth. Cook for half an hour. Add rice and when it is cooked, remove the saucepan from the fire. Beat the eggs with the lemon juice. Put some broth in the beaten eggs. Add all this mixture to the soup. Stirring continually. Serve hot.

RICE SOUP AVGOLEMONO

SOUPA RIZI AVGOLEMONO

Preparation time 30 minutes For 4 persons

1/2 cup rice
5 cups water or meat broth
2 eggs, 1 lemon juice, salt and pepper

    Put the water or the meat broth in pan and bring to boil. Add the rice, salt and pepper and boil for 20 minutes. Remove from the fire. Beat the eggs very well, add the lemon juice little by little. Take some juice of the soup, add it to the eggs, mixing continuously. Pour the mixture in the soup and mix well. Serve hot.

POTATO SOUP

PATATOSOUPA

Preparation time 50 minutes For 5 persons

1 kilo (36 OZ, or 2 lb) potatoes
1 cup onions cut in round pieces
6 cups water
2 cups warm milk
3 table spoons butter, salt and white pepper

MIXED FISH SOUP

PSAROSOUPA ANAMIKTI

Preparation time 50 minutes For 5 persons

1 kilo (36 OZ, or 2 lb) variety of small fish
4 red tomatoes
2 bay leaves
2 medium onions
2 cloves garlic
3 stalks celery
3 medium carrots
1 medium potato
1 cup rice
2 small squash
1 cup olive oil
1 lemon juice, salt and pepper

PILAF

PILAF WITH LIVER

PILAFI ME SIKOTAKIA

Preparation time 60 minutes For 8 persons

1/2 kilo (1 lb, or 18 OZ) chopped liver
750gr. (1 3/4 lb, or 27 OZ) ripe tomatoes pureed
5 table spoons butter
1/2 kilo (1 lb or 18 OZ) rice
1 kilo (2 lb, or 36 OZ) water or meat broth
1 chopped onion
(100gr. 1/4 lb, or 4 OZ) white wine, salt and pepper.

Peel the potatoes and the onions, wash and cut them in pieces. Boil them with water until soft. Drain and grind them. Put the pulp in a saucepan and put it on a low fire. Add salt and pepper, warm milk and mix very well until creamy. Remove from the fire, add the butter and mix until it is soft. Serve hot.

Clean and wash the fish very well. Put them in a saucepan and cover them with salty water. Boil for 20 minutes. Clean, wash and cut the vegetables and put them with the fish. After 20 minutes take the fish out of the saucepan and let the vegetables continue boiling. Clean the fish of their bones and cut them in small pieces. When the vegetables are cooked, drain them, put the broth in the saucepan again on the fire. Add the rice in the broth, as soon as it starts boiling. Grind the vegetables and the fish. Add their pulp in the boiling broth, add olive oil, lemon, pepper and boil until the rice is cooked. Remove from the fire and serve hot.

Wash and cut the liver into very small pieces. In a saucepan, put 3 table spoons, (of the 5), butter to melt. Add the onion to lightly brown, liver and after 5 minutes add the wine, little by little. Add the ground tomatoes, salt and pepper, and let them cook until the sauce becomes thick.

To make the pilaf: In a saucepan put the water or the broth, salt and bring to a boil. Wash the rice many times, and add it to the boiling water. Boil it for 15 minutes. Melt the rest of butter. Add it to the rice. Mix and serve hot.

BAKED PILAF

PILAFI STO FOURNO

Preparation time 45 minutes For 6 persons

2 cups (416gr., or 1 lb, or 15 OZ) rice
4 table spoons butter
1 tea spoon thyme
1 medium chopped onion
5 cups (1050gr, or 2 lb, or 38 OZ)water, salt and pepper

Wash and drain the rice. Melt the butter in a saucepan. Add the onion and saute. Add the rice, thyme, salt and pepper and mix for 5 minutes. Add water mix well and put all, in a baking pan for 20 minutes until cooked. Serve warm in serving dish.

SNAILS WITH RICE

SALIGARIA PILAFI

Preparation time 60 minutes For 6 persons

1/2 kilo (1 lb, or 18 OZ) small snails
2 cups (416gr, or 1 lb, or 15 OZ) rice
1/2 kilo (1 lb, or 18 OZ) ripe tomatoes pureed
1 medium chopped onion, salt and pepper
1 cup olive oil

Choose small snails. Clean and wash them. Boil them in salty water for 15 minutes. (See boiled snails in appetizers). Remove foam which accumulates while boiling. Drain and wash off very well. In another saucepan put the olive oil, onion and tomato puree to saute. Add the snails, mix and let them cook for 10 minutes. Add the rice, salt and pepper, mix for 3 minutes, add 4 cups water and cook for 15 to 20 minutes, until the food will be with no water. Serve warm.

SPINACH RICE

SPANAKORIZO

Preparation time 60 minutes For 6 persons

1/2 kilo (1 lb, or 18 OZ) spinach
2 cups (416gr, or 18 OZ, or 1 lb) rice
3/4 of cup (144gr, or 5 OZ, or 1/4 lb) olive oil
1 large chopped onion, salt and pepper

Wash and cut the spinach into small pieces. In a saucepan put the olive oil, onion and spinach. Mix them until faded. Add salt, pepper and 2 cups of water, cover and cook for 40 minutes. If there is not enough water in the pan, add 1 1/2 cup more, let it boil, add the rice, mix well and let it cook. When rice is done remove from the flame and serve warm.

VEGETABLES WITH PILAF

PILAFI ME LAHANIKA

Preparation time 45 minutes For 6 persons

1 1/2 cup rice (312gr. or 11 OZ, or 3/4 lb)
100gr. (1/4 lb, or 4 OZ) frozen green peas
100gr. (1/4 lb, or 4 OZ) chopped squash
100gr. (1/4 lb, or 4 OZ) carrots
4 table spoons chopped cheese
3 table spoons butter
6 cups water or meat broth (and 2 more if is needed)
salt and pepper

FILAF WITH TOMATOES

RIZI ME DOMATES

Preparation time 90 minutes For 6 persons

2 cups (416gr., or 1 lb, or 15 OZ) rice
1 kilo (2 lb, or 36 OZ) ripe tomatoes pureed
1 large chopped onion
1 cup (192gr. or 1/2 lb, or 7 OZ) olive oil
2 table spoons butter
3 stalks chopped parsley
4 cloves garlic, salt and pepper

PILAF WITH EGG AND LEMON SAUCE

PILAFI ME SALTSA AVGOLEMONO

Preparation time 60 minutes For 8 persons

2 1/2 cups (320gr, or 3/4 lb, or 11 OZ) rice
8 cups water or meat broth, salt

For the sauce:

1 cup (170gr, or 1/2 lb, or 6 OZ) milk
4 table spoons flour
1 cup chopped cheese
4 table spoons butter
Juice of 1 lemon
1 table spoon fresh butter
2 egg yolks, beaten

Wash and cut the vegetables into small cubes. Put in a saucepan the salted water (or the broth) and bring to a boil. Add the green peas, squash, carrots and boil for 15 minutes. Add after the rice and boil for 15 minutes more. Taste the rice if is cooked remove from the fire. Melt the butter. Add the chopped cheese in the pilaf, with the butter and mix well. Serve warm in serving dish.

Put in a saucepan, the olive oil, onion, tomatoes, parsley, garlic, salt and pepper and cook for 30 minutes. Remove from the fire and grind the sauce. Put on the fire again to thicken. Remove from the fire. In an other saucepan put 4 cups salted water and bring to a boil. Add the rice and cook for 20 minutes. Melt the butter, and add it in the rice. Mix well and serve warm in serving dish. Top with the sauce.

In a saucepan put 7 of the 8 cups water or broth and bring to a boil. Wash the rice, and add it in the water. Mix and cook for 20 minutes. Remove from the fire.

In a saucepan warm the milk. Melt the butter, add flour little by little, mixing continuously. Add the 1 cup water or meat broth you have kept aside and mix until thickens and creamy. Remove from the fire, add the beaten egg yolks, with the lemon juice. Put on a low fire for 5 to 7 minutes. Remove, add the half cheese and the fresh butter mixing well. Serve in serving dish warm. Put the rice and cover it with the sauce. Add remaining cheese.

SHRIMPS PILAF

PILAFI ME GARIDES

Preparation time 100 minutes For 8 persons

1/2 kilo (1 lb, or 18 OZ) shrimps
1/2 kilo (1 lb, or 18 OZ) rice
2 large onions
1/2 kilo (1 lb, or 18 OZ) ripe tomatoes
1 cup olive oil
6 cups water from the boiled shrimps, salt and pepper

Wash the shrimps and boil them with water, and the one onion whole, for 25 minutes. Drain and keep the water. Shell the shrimps and put them in a saucepan.

In the same saucepan, put the olive oil, the other onion chopped, and let them cook for 5 minutes. Add the ground tomatoes and cook for 10 minutes. Take out the shrimps, add in the same saucepan, the water you have kept from the shrimps and let it boil. Add the rice, salt and pepper, mix well and boil for 20 minutes. Add the shrimps to the rice, mix well and cook for 5 minutes. Remove from the fire, and set aside 10 minutes before serving.

PILAF WITH GROUN MEAT

PILAFI ME KIMA

Preparation time 60 minutes For 8 persons

1/2 kilo (1 lb, or 16 OZ) ground meat
1 cup olive oil
1/2 cup white wine
1/2 kilo (1 lb, or 16 OZ) ripe tomatoes pureed
1 chopped onion
1 table spoon chopped parsley
1/2 kilo (1 lb, or 18 OZ) rice, salt and pepper

In a saucepan put the olive oil, ground meat, onion and cook for 5 minutes. Add the wine and wait 5 more minutes. Add the pureed tomatoes, the parlsey, salt and pepper, cook for a little while and after add 1 cup water, cook the ground meat for 30 minutes until liquid has been absorbed. In an other saucepan, put 5 cups salty water to boil. Wash the rice. Add it in. Boil for 25 minutes until water has been absorbed. Melt the butter. Add it to the rice. Serve warm the rice and ground meat in serving plate.

PILAF WITH CABBAGE

PILAFI ME LAHANO

Preparation time 60 minutes For 4 persons

1 1/2 cup rice
200gr. (1/2 lb, or 7 OZ) chopped cabbage
1 chopped onion
250gr. (1/2 lb, or 9 OZ) water
6 slices of bacon
1 medium red bell pepper chopped
3 table spoons butter for the cabbage
2 table spoons butter for the rice, salt and pepper

MACARONI AND OTHER PASTRIES

ELBOW MACARONI WITH FRAGRANT SAUCE

MAKARONAKI KOFTO ME SALTSA MIRODADI

Preparation time 50 minutes For 4 persons

300gr. (3/4 lb, or 11 OZ) elbow macaroni
1 bouillon cube (Meat broth)
2 onions
4 table spoons chopped cheese
3 table spoons butter
2 table spoons butter
1 table spoons thyme
2 table spoons beer, salt and pepper

In a saucepan melt the 3 table spoons butter. Add the onion, bacon cuten in small pieces and the bell pepper. Cook for 10 minutes. Add the chopped cabbage with the water, salt and pepper. Mix, and cook in strong fire for 25 minutes. Remove from the fire. In an other saucepan, put 5 cups of water and bring to a boil. Wash the rice. Add it in, and boil around 20 minutes until water is absorbed. Melt the 2 table spoons butter add it to the rice. Put the rice in the cabbage sauce, mix well. Serve warm in serving dish.

Boil the macaroni in salty water. In an other saucepan, melt 3 table spoons butter. Add the onions cut in round slices and lightly brown. Add the beer, thyme, bouillon cube, salt and pepper. Mix well and cook for 15 minutes. Remove from the fire. Drain the macaroni. Add them to the sauce. Melt 2 table spoons butter. Add it to the macaroni, mix and serve warm with the cheese.

MACARONI WITH GREEN REA AND BECHAMEL SAUCE

MACARONIA ME ARAKA KE SALTSA BESAMEL

Preparation time 90 minutes For 4 persons

1 portion regular bechamel sauce
300gr. (3/4 lb, or 11 OZ) frozen green peas
300gr. (3/4 lb, or 11 OZ) macaroni
1 cup chopped ham
2 table spoons butter
4 table spoons chopped cheese
3 table spoons water, salt and pepper

Prepare the bechamel sauce (see in sauces-bechamel regular). Add in, the cheese and ham. In an other saucepan melt the butter, add the green peas, water, salt. Coof for 20 minutes. Then add bechamel. Boil the macaroni in salty water for 20 minutes. Drain and mix them with the bechamel sauce. Mix well and serve warm.

MACARONI WITH POULTRY LIVER

MAKARONIA ME SIKOTAKIA POULIOU

Preparation time 90 minutes For 6 persons

1/2 kilo (1 lb or 18 OZ) macaroni
1/2 kilo (1 lb, or 18 OZ) poultry livers
3 table spoons butter
1 cup chopped cheese
1 cup grated parmezan cheese
3 eggs
4 table spoons fresh butter, salt and pepper

Wash and cut the livers in small pieces. Melt the 3 table spoons of butter. Add to it, the livers, with some salt and cook for 15 minutes. Remove from the fire. Boil the macaroni in salty water for 20 minutes. Drain and wash off and put them again in the saucepan with the 2 of the 4 table spoons the saucepan with the 2 of the 4 table spoons fresh butter. Mix well to melt the butter.

Butter a baking pan and put half the macaroni in, on which you add half the parmezan, mix, add over this the livers. Add the remaining macaroni and mix with the rest parmezan. Beat the eggs, add the chopped cheese over the macaroni. Pour the 2 table spoons fresh butter melted (you haved reserved) and bake in an oven for 20 to 30 minutes until browned. Let it cool. Serve.

BAKED MACARONI

MAKARONIA STO FOURNO

Preparation time 60 minutes For 8 persons

1 kilo (2 lb, or 36 OZ) macaroni
1 1/2 cup chopped cheese
1/2 kilo (1 lb, or 18 OZ) ripe tomatoes
1/2 cup butter, salt and pepper

BAKED MACARONI WITH SHRIMPS

MAKARONIA ME GARIDES STO FOURNO

Preparation time 100 minutes For 6 persons

1/2 kilo (1 lb, or 18 OZ) macaroni
1 kilo (2 lb ,or 36 OZ) shrimps
1/2 kilo (1 lb, or 18 OZ) ripe tomatoes
1/2 cup chopped parsley
1 cup olive oil
1 green bell pepper chopped
100gr. (1/4 lb, or 4 OZ) white wine
1/2 cup chopped onion
2 table spoons butter, salt and pepper.

SQUARE NOODLES WITH CROUN MEAT

HILOPITTES ME KIMA

Preparation time 60 minutes For 4 persons

400gr. (1 lb, or 15 OZ) square egg noodles
1/2 kilo (1 lb, or 18 OZ) minced meat
1 medium chopped onion
1/2 kilo (1 lb, or 18 OZ) ripe tomatoes
1 cup olive oil
2 table spoons butter, salt and pepper

Melt the butter and put it in a baking pan. Grind the tomatoes. Add them to the baking pan, add salt and pepper, 4 cups water and let them cook in the oven for 20 minutes. Add the macaroni mix them very well and baked for 25 minutes. Serve warm with chopped cheese.

Note: The pasta is made the same way in the oven or youvetsi (olzo).

Wash the shrimps and put them in boiling salted water. Boil for 15 minutes, drain and shell them. Cut in small pieces. In an other saucepan add the olive oil with the onion and brown lightly. Add the ground tomatoes, wine, parsley, belle pepper, 2 cups water, salt and pepper.

Boil until this starts to thicken. Add the shrimps let cook for 10 minutes and remove from the fire.

In an other saucepan boil salted water. Add the macaroni. Boil until cooked, 15 to 20 minutes. Drain and wash off. Add them to the shrimps and mix well. Butter a baking pan and put the food in it. Pour 2 table spoons melted butter over it, and bake for 20 to 25 minutes in medium oven. Serve warm.

In a saucepan, put the olive oil, onion ground tomatoes and ground meat. Saute. Add 2 cups water and cook on low fire until liquid is absorbed. Remove from the fire. In an other saucepan put enough salted water and bring to a boil. Add the square noodles, boil for 25 minutes. Drain. Melt the butter, and add it to them. Serve the square noodles with ground meat served on top.

Note: The same way is made and the macaroni with ground meat.

RAVIOLIA

RAVIOLIA

Preparation time 160 minutes For 8 persons

Paste to make the raviolia:

5 cups flour
3 eggs
1 egg white beaten
1 table spoon olive oil
1 table spoon salt
warm water as needed

Stuffing for the raviolia:

1 kilo (2 lb, or 36 OZ) minced meat
1/2 kilo (1 lb, or 18 OZ) ripe tomatoes
1 chopped onion
1/2 cup butter
1 egg, salt and pepper
1/2 cup chopped cheese

The sauce for the raviolia:

1/2 kilo (1 lb, or 18 OZ) ripe tomatoes pureed
1 whole onion, 1 stick cinnamon
6 table spoons butter
salt and pepper

PASTY NUTS WITH CUTTLEFISH SAUCE

ZIMARIKO VITHOULES ME SALTSA APO SOUPIES

Preparation time 60 minutes For 6 persons

1/2 kilo (1 lb, or 18 OZ) pasty nuts
1/2 kilo (1 lb, or 18 OZ) ripe tomatoes
1/2 cup olive oil, 1 chopped onion, 4 slices garlic
1/2 kilo (1 lb, or 18 OZ) cuttlefish, salt and pepper

Paste:

Put the flour in a big bowl. Dissolve the salt in warm water. Add the oil to the flour and mix well. Beat the eggs, add them to the flour, add the salted water, and mix them until it is paste. Let this staid half an hour. Roll into pastry sheets (phyllo) 1/2 inch thick, and cut it in round or square pieces.

Stuffing:

In a saucepan put the butter, minced meat, onion, ground tomatoes, salt and pepper and cook over a low fire for 20 minutes, until liquid is absorbed. Remove from the fire, add the beaten egg, and the cheese, mix all together very well. With a tea spoon add some stuffing to the pastry sheets you have just cut into round or square pieces. Fold in the sides and with a fork, press along edges. Beat the white of the egg which you have keep, when you make the paste.

Brush them with the egg white. Put them in a saucepan with salted water and boil them 20 to 25 minutes. Drain and put them in the saucepan again.

Sauce:

Melt the 2 table spoons butter (of the 6) and pour over the raviolia. In a saucepan put the ground tomatoes the whole onion, cinnamon, salt and pepper and bring to a boil until sauce thickens. Add the rest 4 table spoons butter and mix very well. Serve the raviolia warm with the sauce, and grated cheese on top.

In a saucepan, put the olive oil, onion and garlic. Saute. Clean the cuttlefish, removed the entrails and the ink bag, eyes and bones and rinse thoroughly. Cut into small pieces. Add them to the olive oil.

Add the ground tomatoes, salt and pepper and cook for 40 minutes. In an other saucepan boil enough salted water. Add the pasty nuts in, to boil for 10 to 15 minutes. Drain. Serve them warm with the cuttlefish sauce over them.

BAKED MACARONI WITH MINCED MEAT

MAKARONIA PASTITSIO ME KIMA

Preparation time 90 minutes For 4 persons

1/2 kilo (1 lb, or 18 OZ) thick macaroni
300gr. (3/4 lb, or 11 OZ) chopped cheese and 4 table spoons more.
1/2 kilo (1 lb, or 18 OZ) minced meat
100gr. (1/4 lb, or 4 OZ) white wine
1 cup butter
1 chopped onion
1 stick cinnamon
1/2 kilo (1 lb, or 18 OZ) ripe tomatoes
1 cup bread crumbs
2 egg whites
salt and pepper
1 portion bechamel regular (see in sauces)

In a saucepan put enough salted water and bring to a boil. Add the macaroni and cook for 20 minutes. Drain. Melt half the butter and pour in the macaroni. Beat the white of the eggs very well and mix them with the macaroni. Add half of the cheese and mix very well.

Prepare the minced meat. In a saucepan put the rest of the melted butter. Add the onion. Saute. Add the minced meat, the wine little by little. After a few minutes add the tomatoes puree, cinnamon, salt and pepper, cook for half an hour until liquid is absorbed. Remove from the fire. Add in the minced meat, the rest of the cheese, and half of the bread crumbs. Mix very well. Prepare the bechamel sauce.

Butter a medium bakepan. Put in, half the macaroni. Lay them well in the pan. Over them lay the minced meat. Over it lay the rest macaroni and over them pour the bechamel sauce. Sprinkle with the 4 table spoons chopped cheese, the remaining bread crumbs, and the melted butter. Bake in a medium oven for half an hour until golden brown. Serve warm.

MACARONI WITH ASPARAGUS

MAKARONIA ME SPARANGIA

Preparation time 60 minutes For 6 persons

1/2 kilo (1 lb, or 18 OZ) macaroni
100gr. (1/4 lb, or 4 OZ) chopped ham
1/2 kilo (1 lb, or 18 OZ) asparagus
1/2 cup chopped cheese you prefer
100gr. (1/4 lb, or 4 OZ) butter
salt and pepper, water as needed

MACARONI WITH HAM

MAKARONIA ME ZAMBON

Preparation time 90 minutes For 6 persons

1/2 kilo (1 lb, or 18 OZ) macaroni
3/4 of the cup melted butter
1 cup chopped cheese
3/4 of the cup milk
1 1/2 cup chopped ham
3 eggs
2 table spoons melted butter
1 cup bread crumbs
salt, and pepper

PIES WITH PASTRY SHEETS (PHYLLO)
OR PASTE

Wash the asparagus very well and scrape their skin. Take some pieces, tied them with thread, to make a small bunch. Put them standing in a saucepan in which contains boiling salted water and bring to a boil for 20 minutes. Drain, keeping the water. Cut asparagus in small pieces. In a saucepan melt half the butter, add the asparagus, and after 5 minutes, add the ham, 3 table spoons cheese, salt and pepper, mix together very well. Cook 5 minutes and remove from the fire. In the water which you boil the asparagus, add some more water and boil it. Add the macaroni. Drain and pour with the rest melted butter. Serve the macaroni with the sauce over and chopped cheese on top.

Boil the macaroni in plenty of salted water. Drain and pour with the melted butter. Add half cheese and the ham and mix well. Butter a small baking pan. Put in the macaroni. Beat the eggs, add the milk to them, little by little and the rest cheese. Add all this mixture to the macaroni. Add bread crumbs, the 2 table spoons melted butter and sprinkle over macaroni. Bake in the oven for half an hour until brown.

Serve warm.

Pies are tasty foods. They are made of meat or vegetables and miscelleous spices and seasonings, which give them a nice taste and smell. They are always baked in the oven in a pan. Except the dough, to prepare a pie, we use pastry sheet (phyllo) which we have made or we have bought ready made. The pastry sheets must be soft. For a medium pan 12 pastry sheets are needed. Before the dough or the phyllo is laid, the pan must be grased with olive oil or butter. To butter the phyllo you must use a small brush. Each phyllo must be laid good, not crumpled or broken, and must cover the sides of the baking pan. At the bottom, lay 2-3 more pastry sheets. When adding the filling, the pastry sheets which protrude, fold over the filling. They must be buttered because they will stick together. Cut the pastry sheets which protrude around the pan. Brush them with butter and water, so they will not raise while baking. Score the pie in squares lightly. After baking it, must be set aside about 30 minutes to coagulate. Then serve.

HOME MADE PASTRY SHEETS (PHYLLO) FOR CHEESE

SPINACH PIE WITH CHEESE AND EGGS

SPANAKOPITA ME TIRI KE AVGA

Preparation time 120 minutes 10 parts

1 1/2 kilo (3 lb, or 54 OZ) spinach
1/2 cup fresh chopped scallions
1/2 cup milk
1/2 cup chopped parsley
1/2 cup chopped dill stalks
1 large chopped onion
1 cup butter
5 eggs, salt and pepper
250gr. (1/2 lb, or 9 OZ) feta cheese
12 pastry sheets (phyllo) ready made

FILLO SPITIKO GIA TIROPITES

Preparation time 20 minutes Use after 2 hours

1 cup olive oil
1 cup hot water
self raising flour, water as needed, salt

SQUASH PIE WITH CHEESE

KOLOKITHOTIROPITA

Preparation time 180 minutes For 10 persons

1 1/2 kilo (3 lb, or 54 OZ) squash
1/2 cup milk
1/2 cup bread crumbs
1 cup butter
2 table spoons chopped parsley
2 table spoons chopped dill
5 eggs, salt and pepper
10 pastry sheets ready made
250gr. (1 lb, or 9 OZ) feta cheese

Clean and wash the spinach. Cut it in small pieces. In a saucepan melt the butter, add the chopped onion, fresh onions and the spinach to saute. Mix well. Add the parsley, dill, salt, pepper, and cover to cook, until liquid is absorbed. Remove from the fire. Add the milk to the spinach to cool a little. Beat the eggs, add the cheese cut in pieces. When spinach has cooled completely, add the eggs with the cheese and mix very well. Butter a medium baking pan. Lay 8 pastry sheets buttering each one. Put on the sheets the spinach. Fold the sides of the pastry sheets on the spinach and butter the remaining pastry sheets, and lay them on top of the spinach. Cut the pastry sheets which protrude. Sprinkle with butter and bake in warm oven for 40 to 50 minutes. Let it stand for half an hour to cool. Serve.

Put the flour in a bowl. Make a hole in the middle of it, and add the olive oil, water and salt. Knead to make a soft paste. Add water, or flour if needed. Let stand for 2 hours and after roll out the pastry sheet you want.

You can use ready made pastry sheets (phyllo) for saving time.

Note: All the pies are baked in an oven which must be preheated.

Clean, wash and scrape the squash in the grater. Put them in strainer to strain the excess water.

Let stand approximately 45 minutes. Cut the cheese in thick pieces. Melt half the butter, add the squash and saute. Being careful not to brown. Add salt and pepper, and remove from the fire. Beat the eggs. Add to the beaten eggs the cheese, parsley, dill, bread crumbs, milk, and put this mixture in the squash. Mix very well. Butter a medium baking pan, and lay 8 pastry sheets in the bottom, buttering each one. Put the filling on pastry sheets. Fold the sides over the filling, butter the rest pastry sheets and lay them on the squash. Cut those which protrude. Sprinkle with butter, and bake in a medium oven for 1 hour. Let the pie cool, for half an hour and then serve.

MEAT PIE

KREATOPITA

Preparation time 145 minutes 10 parts

1 kilo (2 lb, or 36 OZ) leg of lamb or leg from beef
2 table spoons chopped parsley
1 tea spoon ground mint
1/2 kilo (1 lb, or 18 OZ) ripe tomatoes
1 cup chopped cheese
1 cup butter
2 raw eggs beaten and 2 hard boiled eggs
4 cloves garlic
1 chopped onion
12 pastry sheets ready made, salt and pepper

PIES WITH FRESH ONIONS AND CHICKEN

PITTES ME FRESKA KREMIDAKIA KE KOTOPOULO

Preparation time 60 minutes For 20 medium parts

400gr. (1 lb, or 15 OZ) boiled or roasted chicken meat
2 table spoons chopped fresh onion
750gr. (1 1/2 lb, or 27 OZ) pastry ready made or pastry you make
1 egg, salt and pepper

PIE WITH MINCED MEAT

PITA ME KIMA

Preparation time 120 minutes 10 parts

1 kilo (2 lb, or 36 OZ) minced meat
1 chopped onion
1/2 kilo (1 lb, or 18 OZ) ripe tomatoes, ground
1 table spoon chopped parsley
2 cups milk
5 eggs, salt and Pepper
1 cup grated cheese
stick of cinnamon
2 toast bread
3/4 of the cup butter

Clean, wash and chop the onion, garlic, parsley. Boil the 2 eggs until hard, and cut them into thin round slices. Cut the meat in small cubes, and add it with the onion and the butter in a sauce pan. Cook for 5 minutes. Add the ground tomatoes, garlic, parsley, mint, salt and pepper and cook in low fire for half an hour. Remove from the fire, add the beaten eggs and the cheese, mix well. Butter a medium baking pan. Butter the pastry sheets singlety and lay 9 of them in the baking pan. Put the filling on them, fold the sides over the filling. Butter the remaining pastry sheets and lay them on top of the filling. Cut pastry pieces which protrude. Sprinkle with butter and bake in a medium oven for 1 hour. Allow to stand half an hour to cool. Serve.

The left over chicken must be boiled or roasted. Chop and grind it. Add the onion, salt and pepper and mix well. Cut the pastry in lengthwise or rounded pieces. Put on pastry pieces one table spoon filling add one other piece of pastry sheet over the filling, brush pastry with beaten egg. Fold and attach the sides so they do not separate while baking. Bake in warm oven for 20 minutes. Serve warm.

In a saucepan melt the half butter. Add the onion, minced meat, ground tomatoes, parsley salt, pepper and cinnamon. Cook for 20 minutes until all the liquid has been absorved. Remove from the fire.

Put the toast bread in the milk to soften. Add this, to the minced meat. Beat the eggs, adding them to the minced meat, add the cheese. Take out the cinnamon, and mix well. Butter each one of the 9 (pastry sheets) and lay them in buttered baking pan. Put the filling on the sheets and fold the sides over the filling. Lay the remaining pastry sheets, buttering each one before adding over the filling, sprinkle with butter and water and bake in a medium oven for 40 minutes. Let stand for half an hour to cool. Serve.

CHEESE PIES WITH YOGURT

TIROPITES ME YIAOURTI

Preparation time 90 minutes 20 parts

Filling:

1 kilo (2 lb, or 36 OZ) hard feta cheese
2 eggs
2 table spoons butter

Paste:

250gr. (1/2 lb, or 9 OZ) plan yog
250gr. (1/2 lb, or 9 OZ) butter
2 egg yolks (reserving the white)
4 cups (512gr., or 1 1/4 lb, or 19
flour

CHICKEN PIE

KOTOPITA

Preparation time 160 minutes For 10 persons

1 medium chicken (around 3 lb, or 54 OZ)
1/2 cup milk
1 cup grated cheese
1 cup butter (224gr., or 8 OZ, or 1/2 lb)
5 eggs
1/2 kilo (1 lb, or 18 OZ) onions
1 cup nutmeg, salt and pepper
12 pastry sheets (phyllo) ready made
1 cup melted butter for the pastry sheets

BRAINS FILLED ROLLS

BOUREKAKIA ME MIALA

Preparation time 120 minutes 20 parts

Bechamel:

1 cup hot milk
2 egg yolks
2 table spoons butter
4 table spoons flour
salt and pepper

Filling:

12 pastry sheets (phyllo) ready made
4 table spoons melted butter for the pastry sheet
1/2 cup grated cheese
1 cup boiled and chopped brains

84

Cut the feta cheese in small pieces and mix it with the eggs and the butter. Mix well. In a bowl put the flour, melted butter, yogurt and the egg yolks. Knead very well. (If the dough needs more flour add some) to make a soft dough. Roll pastry sheets 1/2 inch thick and cut into round or square pieces. Put a table spoon filling on each piece, fold it, and press it to attach at the sides. Brush with the beaten egg whites and bake in medium oven for 20 to 30 minutes   to lightly brown. (Must butter the baking pan before lay pastry sheets in).

Clean, cut and wash the chicken. Boil it in salted water. Slam the foam, add the onions which have been cut in thin slices. Boil well. When chicken is cooked, drain it of the water, and let the onions continue boiling until dissolved. Debone the chicken, taking off the skin and bones. Cut it in small pieces. Add the milk into the boiling onions and boil for 5 minutes   longer. Remove from the fire, add the chicken, cheese, beaten eggs, salt, pepper and nutmeg. Mix well.

. Butter 8 pastry sheets (phyllo) each one and lay them in a medium buttered baking pan. Add the filling, fold the sides of the pastry sheets over the filling. Butter the remaining pastry sheets and lay them on top of the filling. Sprinkle with butter and water and bake in medium oven for 1 hour. Let pie cool for half an hour. Serve.

Make the bechamel sauce (refer to sauces). Put the brains in tepid water for 10 to 20 minutes, remove the blood and the membrane. Put them in salted boiling water for 10 minutes. Drain and cool. Chop them. Put them in a bowl, add the bechamel, sauce, cheese and mix well. Cut the pastry sheets in strips 6 inch width, brush with melted butter, put one table spoon filling at the bigining of the pastry sheet and roll in triangles. Butter a baking pan, lay them in, and bake in medium oven for 15 minutes. Serve hot. (Brush them with butter before baking).

SHRIMP FILLED ROLLS

BOUREKIA ME GARIDES

Preparation time 120 minutes 20 parts

Bechamel:

2 eggs
1 cup milk
3 table spoons grated cheese
4 table spoons flour
3 table spoons butter, salt and pepper

Filling:

10 pastry sheets (phyllo) ready made
4 table spoons melted butter for the pastry sheets
2 table spoons olive oil
3 table spoons chopped parsley
2 onions chopped
1 1/2 cup boiled and chopped shrimps

HAM AND ARTICHOKE FILLED ROLLS

BOUREKIA ME ZABON KE AGINARES

Preparation time 90 minutes 40 pieces

Bechamel:

3 eggs
12 table spoons flour
4 cups milk
1/2 cup butter

Filling:

10 artichokes and 1 lemon
1/2 kilo (1 lb, or 18 OZ) pastry sheets (phyllo) ready
1 cup chopped ham
1 cup chopped cheese
4 table spoons butter

MISCELLANY CHEESE PIE

TIROPITA ME DIAFORA TIRIA

Preparation time 120 minutes 15 parts

200gr. (1/2 lb, or 7 OZ) margarine
500gr. (1 lb, or 18 OZ) yogurt plain
4 eggs
250gr. (3/4lb, or 9 OZ) feta cheese, hard
200gr. (1/2 lb, or 7 OZ) roquefort cheese
200gr. (1/2 lb, or 7 OZ) cheese you prefer
500gr. (1 lb, or 18 OZ) self raising flour

Prepare the bechamel sauce (see sauces). Boil the shrimps in salted water, cool. Shell and chop shrimps. In a saucepan heat the olive oil. Add the shrimps, parsly and onions, and lightly brown. Remove from the fire and allow to cool. Add them to the bechamel sauce, and mix well. Cut each pastry sheet in two pieces. Butter each one, add some filling, folding the sides, and roll in cylindrical form. Butter a baking pan, and lay them in. Brush them with melted butter. Bake in a medium oven for 20 to 30 minutes. Serve warm.

Prepare the bechamel sauce (see sauces). Clean and wash the artichokes. Put them in salted boiling water in which you have added the juice of 1 lemon.

Boil them until cooked. Drain, cool, and cut them in small cubes. Pour melted butter over them and put them in the bechamel sauce with the ham and the cheese. Mix well. Butter each sheet and cut them 8 inches in width. At the begining of each sheet add, one table spoon filling, folding the sides to the inside. Roll in cylindrical form. Butter a baking pan, and lay them in. Brush them with butter, and bake in medium oven for 20 minutes to lightly brown. Serve warm.

In a bowl put the flour, eggs, margarine, yogurt, and mix together very well. Break all the cheese into pieces. Add to the mixture, and mix very well. Butter a baking pan and put the mixture in. Bake it in medium oven for half an hour to 40 minutes. Pierce pie with a knife or fork to see if it is done. Take out of the oven, cool for half an hour. Seve hot or cold.

LEEK PIE

PRASOPITA

Preparation time 120 minutes 10 parts

1 1/2 kilo (3 lb, or 54 OZ) leeks
1 cup butter (224gr, or 1/2 lb, or 8 OZ)
4 table spoons butter for the pastry sheets (phyllo)
7 eggs
1 1/2 table spoon semolina
1/2 kilo (1 lb, or 18 OZ) feta cheese hard
salt, pepper, 1/2 kilo (1 lb, or 18 OZ) pastry sheets ready made

Clean the leeks, of all their green leaves, and keep only the white part. Cut each one of that part in very small pieces, wash and drain. In a saucepan, melt the butter, add the leeks and saute. Cook until all liquid has been absorved. Remove from the fire and cool.

Graded the cheese. Mix it with the beaten eggs. In a bowl put the leeks, eggs with cheese, semolina, salt and pepper and mix them very well. Butter a medium baking pan. Brush 5 pastry sheets buttering each one and lay them in the pan. Add some leeks and over them brush with a little beaten egg. Lay 2 more pastry sheets buttering each one.

Repeat adding more leeks and some beaten egg. Continue like this until the mixture is all used. Put 4 pastry sheets buttering each one, over the filling, sprinkle with melted butter and water. Bake in a medium oven for half an hour. Let pie cool for half an hour and serve.

VEGETABLES

SNAILS WITH ONIONS STEW

SALIGARIA ME KREMIDIA STIFADO

Preparation time 60 minutes For 6 persons

1 kilo (2 lb, or 36 OZ) small snails store-bought
1 cup olive oil (192gr, or 1/2 lb, or 7 OZ)
1 1/2 kilo (3 lb, or 54 OZ) onions
1/2 kilo (1 lb, or 18 OZ) ripe tomatoes
1 table spoon chopped parsley
salt, pepper, 3 bay leaves
1/2 tea spoon nutmeg powder

STEWED CAULIFLOWER

KOUNOUPIDI YIAHNI

Preparation time 45 minutes For 4 persons

1 1/2 kilo (3 lb, or 54 OZ) cauliflower
1/2 kilo (1 lb, or 18 OZ) ripe ground tomatoes
1 cup olive oil (192gr., or 1/2 lb, or 7 OZ)
1 chopped onion
salt, pepper and water as needed

GREEN SQUASH WITH OLIVE OIL OR STEWED

KOLOKITHAKIA LADERA E YIAHNI

Preparation time 45 minutes For 4 persons

1 1/2 kilo (3 lb, or 54 OZ) squash
1/2 kilo (1 lb, or 18 OZ) ripe tomatoes
1 chopped onion
4 cloves of garlic
1 table spoon chopped parsley
1 cup olive oil
salt, pepper, water as needed

Prepare the snails (see appetizers, boiled snails). Clean, wash, and cut the onions in thick slices. Put them in a saucepan with the olive oil and saute. Add the ground tomateos and let stand for 5 minutes. Add the snails, parsley, bayleaves, nutmeg, salt pepper, and mix very well. Cook over low fire for 20 minutes. Serve warm with fried potatoes.

Clean the cauliflower of its leaves, cut it in pieces, and wash it. Grind the tomatoes. In a saucepan put the olive oil, onion and tomatoes and saute. Add the cauliflower, salt and pepper. Mix and let stand for 5 minutes. Add 1 1/2 cup water and cook just a little sauce remains. Cook over low fire.

Clean and wash the squash. Cut them in 3-4 round pieces. In a saucepan, put the olive oil, onion and tomatoes to saute for 5 minutes. Add the squash, garlic, parsley, 1 cup water, salt, pepper and mix well. Cook for half an hour over low fire, until all liguid has been absorbed. Serve warm.

ARTICHOKES WITH BUTTER AND EGG AND LEMON SAUCE

AGINARES VOUTIROU ME SALTSA AVGOLEMONO

Preparation time 60 minutes For 6 persons

12 artichokes, medium
1 large chopped onion
1 cup chopped carrots
4 fresh chopped scallions
1/2 cup chopped dill
3 lemons, 2 eggs
1 cup butter
salt, pepper, water as needed

How to clean the artichokes: Clean the artichokes of its small leaves which are on the stem, and the outside hard leaves. Cut them in two, and with a tea spoon remove their fluff. After you clean the leaves of the steam, peel it. Rub all the artichokes with lemon and put them in a bowl, in which you have put salted water and lemon. This is done, so the artichokes will not blacken. If the artichokes are small, use them whole.

Put in a saucepan the butter and the onion and saute. Add two cups water, dill, carrots, fresh onions and saute them too. Add the juice of one lemon and let stand for 5 minutes. Add the artichokes, salt and pepper, water if it is needed to cover the artichokes. Cover the saucepan and cook in medium heat until the food be with little liquid. Beat the eggs, add the second lemon's juice. Take some liquid from the pan and add it in the eggs, little by little, mixing all the time. Remove the food from the fire, add the egg and lemon sauce, shake the saucepan, (don't mix with a ladle and dissolve the artichokes), put pan again on very low fire so the sauce thickens. Serve warm 4 pieces artichokes to each person.

Note: If you want to cook artichokes with olive oil instand of butter use 1 cup olive oil, and do not use egg, but as much lemon as you want. The procedure is exactly the same.

GRILLED ARTICHOKES

AGINARES PSITES STH SHARA

Preparation time 60 minutes For 4 persons

8 medium artichokes
1 lemon
4 table spoons olive oil
1 garlic bulb, salt and pepper

STEWED EGGPLANTS

MELITZANES YIAHNI

Preparation time 45 minutes For 4 persons

BAKED POTATOES WITH CUMIN

PATATES PSITES ME CIMINO

Preparation time 45 minutes For 8 persons

8 potatoes
2 table spoons cumin
1/2 cup butter, salt and pepper

The artichokes must be very fresh. Clean them, without throwing many outside leaves. Cut them in two pieces, and with a tea spoon remove their fluff. Rub them with lemon and put them in boiling salted water for 10 minutes. Drain and cool. Sprinkle with olive oil and bake on the grill, in low oven for 10 minutes, turning to cook of each side. Make olive oil sauce (see sauces) and pour over the artichokes. Clean and grind the garlic to be a pulp.

Pour with the garlic pulp the artichokes and serve warm 4 pieces artichoke to each person. Served with fried fish and mostly with fried salted codfish.

Made exactly like the stewed squash. Nothing is changed neither the portion nor the way of cooking.

Note: Squash and eggplants, can be fried too. Clean wash and cut them in oblong slices, sprinkle with flour in which (flour) you have add some salt, and fry in 2 1/2 cups very hot olive oil, until they are golden brown. Serve warm with garlic sauce (see sauces) or use them as trimmings with roasted meat.

Clean and wash the potatoes. Cut them in 2 pieces length-wise. Put them on the grill, with the cut sides under. Bake them in low oven for 15 to 20 minutes. Turn off the oven. Melt butter and sprinkle some in each potato (on the cut flat side) add the cumin. Serve warm with grilled or baked meat, 2 pieces to each person.

BROAD BEANS WITH OLIVE OIL AND TOMATOES

KOUKIA YAHNI

Preparation time 60 minutes For 4 persons

1 kilo (2 lb, or 36 OZ) broad green beans
3 fresh scallions chopped
2 table spoons chopped dill fresh
2 table spoons chopped parsley fresh
1 table spoon mint powder
1/2 kilo (1 lb, or 18 OZ) ripe ground tomatoes, salt and pepper

BAKED MISCELLANEOUS VEGETABLES

BRIAM

Preparation time 150 minutes For 8 persons

1 kilo (2 lb, or 36 OZ) ripe tomatoes
1/2 kilo (1 lb, or 18 OZ) eggplants
1/2 kilo (1 lb, or 18 OZ) squash
1/2 kilo (1 lb, or 18 OZ) potatoes
250gr. (1/2 lb, or 9 OZ) carrots
250gr. (1/2 lb, or 9 OZ) green pepper-plants cutten in thin round slices
1/2 cup chopped parsley
1/2 cup garlic cloves
1 cup onions cut in thin round slices
2 cups olive oil, salt and pepper

ARTICHOKES WITH POTATOES

AGINARES ME PATATES

Preparation time 60 minutes For 4 persons

8 medium artichokes
1/2 kilo (1 lb, or 18 OZ) small potatoes
2 table spoons chopped dill
1 table spoon chopped parsley
4 cloves of garlic
3 large onions
1 cup olive oil
salt and pepper

Remove the string from the beans and cut their ends. Put in a saucepan the olive oil, onion, dill, parsley, mind and saute. Add the washed broad beans, ground tomatoes, salt, pepper and cook for half an hour over low fire, until be with their sauce. Serve almost warm. (Add water if needed).

Clean, wash, and cut the vegetables in medium slices. Put them in a baking pan. Add the parsley, onions, green pepper and add garlic as it is, add salt, pepper, the olive oil and bake in medium oven for 2 hours. Add two cups water, and more if needed during baking. Serve warm.

Clean the artichokes (see artichokes with butter, for how to clean). Peel the onions and cut them in thin slices. In a saucepan put the olive oil, onions, dill and parsley to saute for 10 minutes. Cut the artichokes in slices. Add them in. Let cook for 10 more minutes. Add the potatoes cut in two halves, garlic and as much water as needed to cover the ingredients. Add salt, pepper and cook until be, with its sauce. Serve warm.

ARTICHOKES AND PEAS WITH OLIVE OIL

AGINARES ME ARAKA LADERES

Preparation time 60 minutes For 6 persons

1 1/2 kilo (3 lb, or 54 OZ) frozen peas
6 artichokes
1/2 kilo (1 lb, or 18 OZ) ripe ground tomatoes
1 chopped onion
1/2 cup chopped dill fresh
1 cup olive oil, salt, pepper, water as needed

OKRA WITH POTATOES AND OLIVE OIL

BAMIES ME PATATES YAHNI

Preparation time 45 minutes For 6 persons

1 1/2 kilo (3 lb, or 54 OZ) frozen okra or a large can
1/2 kilo (1 lb, or 18 OZ) ripe ground tomatoes
1 chopped onion
2 large potatoes, salt and pepper
1 cup olive oil

BROAD BEANS WITH ARTICHOKES

FRESKA KOUKIA ME AGINARES

Preparation time 60 minutes For 6 persons

1 1/2 kilo (3 lb, or 54 OZ) fresh broad beans
6 artichokes
1/2 cup chopped dill fresh
1/2 cup chopped fresh scallions
1/2 cup chopped carrots
1 cup olive oil, salt, pepper, water as needed

Defrost the peas. Clean the artichokes. (See buttered artichokes with lemon and egg sauce, how to clean). In a saucepan put the onion with the olive oil and saute. Add the tomatoes and wait for 5 minutes. Add the peas and artichokes, dill, 1 cup water, salt and pepper, and cook over low fire until be with a thick sauce. Serve warm.

The okra does not neet to be cleaned unless they are fresh. Wash them very well and drain. Remove okra's stems without cutting. Clean well. Sprinkle with vinegar and salt, and lay them in the sun for 2 hours, before cooking.

Clean and wash the potatoes. In a saucepan put the olive oil, with onion and tomatoes and saute. Add the okra with the potatoes cut in 4 pieces. Add salt and pepper, 1 1/2 cup water and cook for half an hour. When the food will be with its sauce, remove from the fire. During the cooking add more water if its needed.

1) If the okra are canned, add them in the saucepan, 10 minutes before the end of cooking.

2) If the canned okra has tomatoes with them omit the 1/2 kilo of tomatoes, in the recipe.

Clean the artichokes. (See artichokes with butter and egg with lemon sauce). Remove the strings of the broad beans and cut their ends. Wash them. In a saucepan put the onions with the olive oil, dill and carrots and saute.

Add the broad beans, artichokes, 2 cups water, salt and pepper and cook over low fire for half an hour, to be with a thick sauce. Add more water if needed. Serve warm.

BAKED MASHED SPINACH

SPANAKI POURE STO FOURNO

Preparation time 50 minutes For 4 persons

1 portion of regular bechamel sauce
1 1/2 kilo (3 lb, or 54 OZ) spinach
3 table spoons butter, 1 egg
4 table spoons grated cheese
1/2 cup bread crumbs
1 tea spoon nutmeg, salt and pepper

STRING BEANS WITH OLIVE OIL AND TOMATOES

FASOLIA FRESKA YAHNI

Preparation time 60 minutes For 4 persons

1 kilo (2 lb, or 36 OZ) green beens
1 chopped onion
1/2 kilo (1 lb, or 18 OZ) ripe ground tomatoes
1 cup olive oil, salt and pepper

SPINACH WITH RICE

SPANAKORIZO

Preparation time 45 minutes For 4 persons

1/2 kilo (1 lb, or 18 OZ) spinach
1 cup rice
1 cup olive oil
1 chopped onion, salt, pepper, water as needed

Clean the spinach, wash it and put it in a saucepan with salted water. Bring to a boil. Prepare the bechamel. (See sauces, bechamel sauce regular). Add in the bechamel sauce, nutmeg and the half grated cheese. Mash the spinach. Add to the bechamel, add the egg, and mix very well. Butter a baking pan and put in the mixture. Cover with the bread crumbs, the remaining cheese, melted butter, and bake in a medium oven for 20 to 30 minutes. Let it cool and serve. Serve with grilled meat or grilled fish.

Clean the fibrils from the beans. Cut them in half if they are very large and wash them. In a saucepan, put the olive oil, with onion and tomateos and saute. Add the fresh beans, salt and pepper, 2 cups water cook, over low fire for half an hour, until they'll be with a thick sauce. Serve almost warm with fried fish or fried potatoes.

Clean the spinach of its yellow leaves, wash and cut it in small pieces. In a saucepan put the olive oil with the onion and saute. Add the spinach sauteing it too, and let it cook until all the liquid has been absorbed, approximately half an hour. Add 2 cups water. When it starts to boil add the rice, salt and pepper, and cook until the rice is done. Mix and serve warm.

FRIED MUSHROOMS

MANITARIA TIGANITA

Preparation time 20 minutes For 6 persons

1/2 cup olive oil, 1 lemon
1/2 kilo (1 lb, or 18 OZ) mushrooms
1 table spoon chopped parsley, salt and pepper

FRIED EGGPLANTS WITH TOMATO SAUCE

MELITZANES TIGANITES ME SALTSA DOMATA

Preparation time 30 minutes For 4 persons

1 1/2 kilo (3 lb, or 54 OZ) eggplants
1/2 kilo (1 lb, or 18 OZ) ripe ground tomatoes
1 chopped onion
1 table spoon chopped parsley fresh
3 cups olive oil
salt, pepper, flour

BAKED GIANT DRY BEANS

FASOLIA GIGANTES PLAKI STO FOURNO

Preparation time 120 minutes For 4 persons

1/2 kilo (1 lb, or 18 OZ) giant dry beans
1/2 kilo (1 lb, or 18 OZ) ripe ground tomatoes
250gr. (1/2 lb, or 9 OZ) green bell peppers
250gr. (1/2 lb, or 9 OZ) onions
1 garlic bulb
1/2 cup chopped parsley fresh
2 cups olive oil, salt and pepper

Clean, wash the mushrooms and cut them in thin slices.

Sprinkle them with the lemon juice. In a frying pan heat the olive oil. Put the mushrooms in and fry them for 15 minutes   over low fire. Add salt and pepper, lemon juice, parsley and serve.

Wash and cut eggplants in oblong slices. Salt and flour them. Heat the olive oil in a frying pan, and fry the eggplants on both sides. When finished with frying the eggplants, add in the same olive oil, the tomatoes, onion, parsley and some pepper and cook until sauce thickens. Pour over the eggplants and serve warm.

Soak the beans in water, (cold) over night. Next day, drain them. In a saucepan, put the beans, cover with water, and boil for 45 minutes. In a baking pan, put the olive oil.

Cut the onions and the green bell-peppers in round thin slices. Add them in the olive oil. Peel the garlic. Add parsley, garlic, onions and mix all these well. Add the boiled beans, salt and pepper and 2 cups water. Bake in a medium oven for half an hour until be with a thick sauce. Serve warm, with fried fish and salad.

MUSHROOMS WITH OLIVE OIL

MANITARIA LADERA

Preparation time 45 minutes For 6 persons

750gr. (1 3/4lb, or 27 OZ) mushrooms
500gr. (1 lb, or 18 OZ) onions
1 cup olive oil
1/2 cup wine
1 lemon, salt and pepper
2 fresh celery stalks - 2 fresh stalks parsley and 2 fresh stalks dill
2 bay leaves (Tie all these together with a piece of thread)

Clean and wash the mushrooms. Cut them in half if they are large. Clean and wash the onions. Cut them in thick slices. Put them in a saucepan with the olive oil and saute. Add 1 cup water, lemon, wine and the spices, salt, pepper. Cook for 25 minutes. Add the mushrooms. Cook for 15 minutes to be with a thick sauce. Remove the spices and serve.

EGGPLANTS IMAM BAYLDI

MELITZANES IMAM BAYLDI

Preparation time 120 minutes For 6 persons

1 1/2 kilo (3 lb, or 54 OZ) oblong medium eggplants
1/2 kilo (1 lb, or 18 OZ) ground ripe tomatoes
3 cups olive oil
4 chopped onions
1 cup chopped parsley, 1 garlic bulb
1/2 cup bread crumbs
1/2 cup grated cheese, salt, pepper

FILLED VEGETABLES AND MOUSAKA

FILLED TOMATOES WITH RICE

DOMATES GEMISTES ME RIZI

Preparation time 145 minutes For 6 persons

1 1/2 cup olive oil and 1/2 cup more
1 cup rice
12 tomatoes medium size
3/4 kilo (1 3/4lb, or 27 OZ) potatoes
1/2 cup bread crumbs
1/2 cup chopped parsley fresh
2 large chopped onions
1/2 tea spoon cumin, salt, pepper

Wash the eggplants. Cut in half, without separating both halves.

Put them in salted water for 15 minutes. Drain, wash well, and wipe them. Put the olive oil in a frying pan to heat and fry them whole on both sides. Put them in a broad large saucepan in rows. In the same olive oil in which you have fried the eggplants, add the onios, garlic, tomatoes, parsley, salt and pepper and fry for 20 minutes   until liquid is absorbed. Remove from the fire. With a tea spoon take sauce and fill the center of eggplants.

Pour some grated cheese and some bread crumbs over them. Put in the saucepan with the rest of the sauce, adding 1/2 cup olive oil, 1 cup water and cook for 45 minutes. Serve warm.

Wash, and wipe the tomatoes. Cut off the stemmed end a thin slice and save it. Remove pulp with a tea spoon. Reserve pulp. Salt the tomatoes inside. Peel and wash the potatoes. Cut in four pieces. Ground the tomato pulp. In a saucepan put, the 1 1/2 cup of olive oil, onion tomatoes pulp and saute them for 5 minutes. Add the rice, with 1 cup water, parsley, cumin, salt, pepper, and cooked until the rice is half done. With a tea spoon take some filling, and put it in the tomatoes. Do not full them. Cover with the tomatoes stems you have saved from the begining and put them in rows, in a baking pan. Add the rest 1/2 cup of olive oil and the bread crumbs on, the tomatoes. Salt the potatoes, and put them between each tomato. Add 1 1/2 cup water, and bake in medium oven for 45 minutes. Serve almost warm 2 pieces of tomatoes to each person.

FILLED ARTICHOKES

AGINARES GEMISTES

Preparation time 120 minutes For 4 persons

12 large artichokes
3/4 of kilo (1 3/4lb, or 27 OZ) ground meat
1/2 cup olive oil
1 chopped onion
1/2 cup grated cheese
1/2 cup bread crumbs
1/2 kilo (1 lb, or 18 OZ) ground ripe tomatoes
1/2 portion bechamel regular sauce
salt, pepper, 4 table spoons melt butter

FILLED EGGPLANTS WITH GROUND MEAT

MELITZANES GEMISTES ME KIMA

Preparation time 145 minutes For 6 persons

1/2 kilo (1 lb, or 18 OZ) ground meat
1 1/2 kilo (3 lb, or 54 OZ) oblong eggplants
1 cup rice
1/2 kilo (1 lb, or 18 OZ) ground ripe tomatoes
1 1/2 cup olive oil
1/2 cup chopped parsley fresh
1/2 cup bread crumbs
salt, pepper, 1 medium chopped onion

Clean the artichokes, cutting the stems and the leaves completely. Do not cut the artichokes. Remove their fluff, and make a small cavity to put the filling in. Rub them with lemon, and put them in salted water, with lemon juice in. When the artichokes are all finished wash off very well and boil them in salted water for 10 minutes. Drain and let them cool. In a saucepan put, the olive oil, onion, tomatoes and let them saute for 5 minutes. Add the ground meat, salt and pepper, mix well and cook for 10 more minutes. Add 1 cup water and let the food cook until all water be absorbed. When its done, take an artichoke, put in some ground meat, add over it 1 table spoon bechamel, add some cheese and some bread crumbs. Continue like this until all the artichokes finished. Butter a baking pan, and put them in. Sprinkle over each artichoke, melted butter and bake in medium oven for 20 minutes, until golden brown. Serve almost warm 3 pieces artichokes to each person.

Clean, wash the eggplants, and cut a piece of the top. Remove the seeds.

Soak them in water. When finish this, drain and boil them in salted water for 15 minutes. Drain very well. In a saucepan put, the olive oil, onions, tomatoes, ground meat and saute. Mix well and let them saute for 5 minutes. Add the parsley, salt, pepper, 1 cup water and cook for 15 minutes. Add 1 cup more water and when it boils, add the rice, which you had washed good. Mix well and cook for 10 to 15 minutes. Take one eggplant, put some filling in, but do not fill it. Put some bread crumbs over it. When finish with all eggplants, put them in buttered baking pan and sprinkle them, with melted butter. Add to the baking pan 1/2 cup warm water. Bake in medium oven for 45 minutes. Wait to cool and serve.

FILLED TOMATOES WITH EGGPLANTS

DOMATES GEMISTES ME MELITZANES

Preparation time 145 minutes For 6 persons

12 tomatoes medium size
4 medium chopped eggplants
1/2 cup rice
1 1/2 cup olive oil
1/2 cup grated cheese
1 big chopped onion
1/2 cup chopped parsley fresh
1/2 cup bread crumbs, salt, pepper

SQUASH FILLED WITH GROUND MEAT

KOLOKITHAKIA GEMISTA ME KIMA

Preparation time 120 minutes For 4 persons

1/2 kilo (1 lb, or 18 OZ) ground meat
1 1/2 kilo (3 lb, or 54 OZ) medium squash
1/2 cup rice
1 chopped onion
2 cups chopped parsley
5 small ripe tomatoes ground
1/2 cup bread crumbs
1/2 cup grated cheese
salt, pepper, water as needed
1 cup butter
2 lemons
2 eggs

Wash the tomatoes, cut off the stemmed end and save it. Empty them of their pulp, salt them inside. Cut the eggplants, clean and chop them, puting immediately in salted water. Put the olive oil in a frying pan and heat it. Drain the eggplants, and flour lightly. Fry them until cooked. Put them in a bowl. Add the rice, parsley, onion, cheese, bread crumbs, tomato pulp, salt and pepper. Mix very well.

Fill each tomato with filling and cover with the stemmed ends you have saved. Put them in a baking pan, add the olive oil in which you had fried the eggplants and 1 cup water. Bake in medium oven for 40 minutes. Serve almost warm, 2 tomatoes to each person.

Clean the squash. Cut off their stemmed ends, and save them. With a tea spoon empty their inners, without cutting it any where. Salt them. In a saucepan put the ground meat, the half butter, onion, tomatoes, parsley, salt, pepper, 1/2 cup water, and cook for 20 minutes. Add 1 cup warm water, and when it boils, add the washed rice. Cook for 10 minutes over low fire. Remove from the fire, add the bread crumbs, cheese and let them cool. Add the well beaten egg whites. Take each squash, and with a tea spoon fill it with the filling. Put them in a saucepan in rows. Melt the rest of the butter. Add it in the saucepan. Add 1 cup water and cook over low fire for 30 minutes. When the squash are done, remove from heat, and pierce them with a fork, to see if they are cooked. Beat the egg yolks, add the lemon in them, some liquid from the food, and mix well and continuously. Add them in the squash, shake the saucepan so the sauce will spread over entire pan, and cook in low fire for 5 to 7 minutes. Serve almost warm.

FILLED TOMATOES WITH EGGS

DOMATES GEMISTES ME AVGA

Preparation time 90 minutes For 4 persons

8 large tomatoes
8 eggs
1 cup butter
2 table spoons chopped parsley

1/2 kilo (1 lb, or 18 OZ) graviera cheese, salt pepper
4 table spoons bread crumbs

FILLED SQUASH WITH RICE

KOLOKITHAKIA GEMISTA ME RIZI

Preparation time 90 minutes For 4 persons

1 1/2 kilo (3 lb, or 54 OZ) squash
1 cup rice
1 cup butter
1 large chopped onion
1/2 cup chopped parsley fresh
1/2 cup bread crumbs
1/2 cup grated cheese
2 lemons, 2 eggs
salt, pepper, water as needed

FILLED TOMATOES WITH GROUNT MEAT

DOMATES GEMISTES ME KIMA

Preparation time 120 minutes For 6 persons

12 large tomatoes
750gr. (1 3/4lb, or 27 OZ) ground meat
3 table spoons chopped parsley
1 large chopped onion
1/2 cup bread crumbs
1/2 cup grated cheese
1/2 cup wine
2 cups olive oil
salt, pepper, cumin

112

Wash the tomatoes, cut off the stemmed end, and save it. Remove their pulp. Salt inside and put some parsley in each one. Cut the cheese, in 8 slices and the remaining cheese grate it. Put inside each tomato some greated cheese.

Put the butter in a baking pan, grind the tomato pulp and put it in the baking pan. Bake in medium oven for 15 minutes. Remove from the oven. With a table spoon take some sauce from the baking pan and put it in the tomatoes. Put on each tomato one cheese slice, and over it put 1 egg. (Not beaten). Put on the egg, salt, pepper, grated cheese, bread crumbs, some olive oil from the baking pan, and put in the oven again. Bake in low fire for 20 minutes. Serve 2 tomatoes to each person.

Prepared exactly like the filled squash with ground meat. The difference is that you are not using the tomatoes, nor the ground meat, but only rice which you will cook with the others, ingredients for 25 minutes. To prepare the sauce with the eggs is exactly the same way, as with ground meat.

Wash the tomatoes, cut off the stemmed end, and save it. Empty them of their pulp. Salt inside the tomatoes. In a saucepan put, the onion, with half the olive oil and saute. Add the ground meat and cook for 5 minutes. Add the wine. Cook 5 more minutes. Add the ground tomato pulp, parsley, salt, pepper, 1 cup water and cook in low fire for 1 hour, until all liquid has been absorbe. Remove from the fire. Add the cheese and the bread crumbs and mix well. With a table spoon take some filling and put it in the tomatoes.

Do not fill them full. Cover with the tomato slices you have saved. Put them in a baking pan, add the rest of the olive oil in, 1/2 cup water and cook in medium oven for 30 to 45 minutes. Serve almost warm.

FILLED EGGPLANTS LITTLE SHOES

MELITZANES PAPOUTSAKIA

Preparation time 120 minutes For 8 persons

8 large round eggplants
1 portion regular bechamel sauce
300gr. (3/4 lb, or 11 OZ) ground meat
2 cups butter or olive oil
1/2 kilo (1 lb, or 18 OZ) ground ripe tomatoes
1/2 cup grated cheese
1 large chopped onion
2 table spoons chopped parsley
1/2 cup bread crumbs, salt, pepper

FILLED TOMATOES WITH ROASTED MEAT

DOMATES GEMISTES ME PSITO KREAS

Preparation time 100 minutes For 6 persons

12 medium tomatoes
3 1/2 cups chopped roast meat
1/2 cup olive oil
1 portion bechamel sauce
2 large chopped onions
2 table spoons chopped celery
1 cup grated cheese
1/2 cup chopped parsley, salt, pepper

Wash the eggplants, wipe and cut them oblong and in halfs. Remove their pulp. Fry the eggplants with butter or olive oil. Do not burn them. When finished frying, put the olive oil in a saucepan. Put the onion in, ground meat, ground tomatoes, parsley, salt and pepper. Cook for half an hour until the food be without liquid. Prepare the bechamel (see regular bechamel sauce, in sauces). Take each eggplant, fill it with ground meat, some bechamel, cheese, and bread crumbs on top. When finished sprinkle with melted butter and put them in baking pan. Bake in medium oven for 20 minutes until lightly brown.

Serve warm with salad.

Wash the tomatoes, cut off the stemmed end, and save it. Remove their pulp. Salt and pepper inside them. Prepare the bechamel (see in sauces, regular bechamel sauce). In a frying pan heat the olive oil. Add the onion, meat, parsley, celery, and ground pulp from the tomatoes, and saute. Add salt pepper and cook for 25 minutes over low fire. Add the half cheese in the bechamel sauce and mix well. Put filling in the tomatoes and cover with bechamel. Pour with cheese, sprinkle with melted butter. Put them in a baking pan and bake in medium oven for 15 minutes until golden brown. Serve warm 2 tomatoes to each person.

GRAPE LEAVES STUFFED WITH GROUND MEAT AND EGG SAUCE

DOLMADES KLIMATOFILA ME KIMA KE SALTSA AVGOLEMONO

Preparation time 120 minutes For 6 persons

750gr. (1 3/4 lb, or 27 OZ) ground meat
1/2 kilo (1 lb, or 18 OZ) grape leaves
1 cup butter
1/2 cup rice
1 large chopped onion
1/2 cup chopped parsley
1 table spoon corn-flour
2 eggs, 2 lemons, salt, pepper, water as needed.

CABBAGE LEAVES STUFFED WITH EGGS AND LEMON SAUCE

DOLMADES LAHANO ME SALTSA AVGOLEMONO

Preparation time 120 minutes For 6 persons

2 kilos (4lb, or 72 OZ) cabbage
750gr (1 3/4lb, or 27 OZ) ground meat
1/2 cup rice
1 large chopped onion
1 table spoon chopped dill fresh
2 table spoons chopped parsley fresh
2 eggs, salt, pepper
1 cup liquid from the food
2 lemons
1 cup milk
1 table spoon corn-flour
1/2 cup butter

Wash the grape leaves very well and put them in boiling water to scald. Drain and cool. In a bowl put, the onion, ground meat, parsley, washed rice, the whites of the eggs, salt and pepper and mix very well. Take each grape leaf from the wrong side and put on it some stuffing. Fold the ends of each leaf on top of the stuffing and roll it up. Put them in a saucepan, next to each other very close and continue like that, until all the grape leaves and the stuffing finish. Add hot water as needed to cover them, the butter and some salt. Cover the grape leaves with a plate to protect them of unwraping during cooking. Cover the saucepan and cook in low fire for half an hour, until the food be with 2 cups liquid. Remove from the fire. Beat the egg yolks, add lemons juice, corn-flour, some pepper, and the food's liquid. Beat all these very well. Add this sauce in the grape leaves. Shake the saucepan with your hands so the sauce will go every where. Cook for 10 minutes in low fire and serve warm.

Clean the cabbage. Separate leaves and wash them very well. Put it in boiling water to scald. Let them cool. Continue this until all the leaves finish. In a bowl put the rice, ground meat, onion, parsley, dill and egg whites, salt and pepper. Mix very well. Take each leaf, cut it if it's big, on the wrong side and put on, some stuffing. Fold the ends of the leaf over the stuffing and roll it up. Put it in a saucepan next to each. Add salt, pepper, warm water to cover the cabbage, melted butter and cover them with a plate. Cover the saucepan and cook on low fire for 60 minutes until it has 1 cup of liquid. Remove from heat. Dissolve the corn-flour in the milk. Beat the egg yolks, add lemon, milk, and the hot liquid. Mix very well. Add the sauce to the cabbage, shake the saucepan with your hands so the sauce spreads, and put on a very low fire for 5 to 10 minutes. Remove from the fire and serve warm.

SQUASH MOUSAKA

KOLOKITHAKIA MOUSAKA

Preparation time 145 minutes For 6 persons

1 1/2 kilo (3 lb, or 54 OZ) squash
3/4 of kilo (1 3/4lb or 27 OZ) ground meat
1 cup butter
1 1/2 cup olive oil for frying
1/2 kilo (1 lb, or 18 OZ) ground ripe tomatoes
1 chopped onion
1/2 cup bread crumbs
3/4 of cup grated cheese
1 portion bechamel sauce, salt, pepper

STUFFED CABBAGE LEAVES WITH WHITE SAUCE

LAHANO DOLMADES ME ASPRI SALTSA

Preparation time 160 minutes For 6 persons

2 kilo (4lb, or 72 OZ) cabbage
250gr. (1/2 lb, or 9 OZ) rice
1 cup olive oil
3/4 of cup butter
1 cup milk
1 large chopped onion
1 table spoon chopped dill fresh
1/2 cup pine-nuts
2 table spoons chopped parsley fresh
2 lemons, 2 eggs, 3 table spoons flour
salt, pepper, water as needed

Clean and wash the squash. Cut them in oblong thin slices. Salt them and fry in the olive oil. In a saucepan, melt half the butter. Add the onion and saute. Add the ground meat, tomatoes, salt, pepper, 1 cup water and cook for half an hour until liquid is absorbed. Remove from the fire. Add half and the bread crumbs. Mix very well. Prepare the bechamel sauce. (See in sauces, bechamel sauce regular). Butter a medium size baking pan. Put the half squash, one next to other in the baking pan. Put over them some cheese and the ground meat. Lay over the ground meat the remaining squash and over them the bechamel sauce. Pour with the remaining cheese and bread crumbs, sprinkle with the rest half melted butter and bake in warm oven for 40 minutes. Let it cool and serve.

Clean the cabbage, separate each one of its leaves and wash it. Put some leaves in boiling water to scald. Be careful not to over cook. Continue this until all the leaves finish. Let them cool. Wash the rice and put it in a bowl. Put in, the onion, parsley, dill, pine-nuts, egg whites, half olive oil, salt and pepper and mix all these very well. Take one cabbage leaf, (cut it in two pieces if it is big) and at the wrong side put some stuff on. Fold the ends of the leaf over the stuffing and roll it up. Put them in a saucepan, next to each. When finished stuffing, put the rest olive oil in, lemon and warm water to cover leaves. Cover them with a plate, and with the top of the saucepan and cook on low fire for 25 minutes. When the food have 1 1/2 cup liquid, remove from the fire. Melt the butter, add the flour in, and mix well. Heat the milk and mix it with the food's liquid. Add them in the butter, mix and cook the sauce to coagulate. Remove from the fire. Beat the egg yolks. Add them to the sauce, put salt and pepper, and mix very well. Pour the sauce on the cabbage leaves, shake the saucepan with your hands, so the sauce will go every where, and put the saucepan on very low fire for 5 to 10 minutes. Serve almost hot.

POTATO, SQUASH, EGGPLANT MOUSAKA

MOUSAKAS ME PATATES, KOLOKITHAKIA KE MELITZANES

Preparation time 180 minutes For 8 persons

1/2 kilo (1 lb, or 18 OZ) squash
1/2 kilo (1 lb, or 18 OZ) potatoes
1/2 kilo (1 lb, or 18 OZ) eggplants
1 1/2 kilo (3 lb, or 54 OZ) ground meat
750gr (1 3/4 lb, or 27 OZ) ground ripe tomatoes
1/2 cup olive oil
4 cups olive oil for frying
6 table spoons butter
1/2 cup chopped parsley fresh
2 large chopped onions
1 cup bread crumbs
1 cup grated cheese
1 cup wine
1 portion bechamel sauce, salt, pepper

Wash the vegetables and cut them in slices. Put salt and pepper. Fry the potatoes first, the squash after, and the eggplants at the end. In a saucepan put the olive oil, onion, tomatoes, ground meat, parsley, salt and pepper and saute for 10 minutes. Add the wine, 1 cup water, and cook for half an hour, until be without liquid at all. Remove from the fire, add in half the cheese and bread crumbs. Prepare the bechamel (see in sauces, bechamel regular sauce). Butter a baking pan and put in, the potatoes one next to the other. Put over them, half the ground meat. Over it put, the squash one next to the other. Put over them the remaining ground meat. Over it put the eggplants. Cover them with the bechamel sauce. Pour over the remaining cheese and bread crumbs. Melt the 6 table spoons butter and sprinkle well. Bake in medium oven for 40 minutes. Let it cool and serve.

Note: All the mousaka, can be served with any salad and cheese you like.

POTATO MOUSAKA

PATATES MOUSAKA

Preparation time 145 minutes For 6 persons

1 1/2 kilo (3 lb, or 54 OZ) potatoes
750gr (1 3/4lb, or 27 OZ) ground meat
3 table spoons butter and 4 more
1 1/2 cup olive oil for frying
1/2 kilo (1 lb, or 18 OZ) ground ripe tomatoes
1 table spoon fresh chopped parsley
1 large chopped onion
1 cup grated cheese
1 cup bread crumbs
1 portion bechamel, salt, pepper

EGGPLANT MOUSAKA

MELITZANES MOUSAKA

Preparation time 145 minutes For 6 persons

750 gr. (1 3/4 lb, or 27 OZ) ground meat
1 1/2 kilo (3 lb, or 54 OZ) eggplants
1/2 kilo (1 lb, or 18 OZ) ground ripe tomatoes
1 large chopped onion
1 table spoon chopped parsley fresh
1 cup bread crumbs
1 cup grated cheese
1/2 cup wine
1 portion bechamel sauce, regular
1 cup olive oil for the ground meat
2 cups olive oil for frying
4 table spoons butter, salt, pepper

Peel the potatoes, wash and cut them in round slices. Heat the olive oil in the frying pan and fry the potatoes. In a saucepan, melt the 3 table spoons butter. Add the onion, ground meat, tomatoes parsley, salt, pepper, 1 cup of water, and cook for half an hour until liquid is absorbed.

Remove from the fire. Add in, half the cheese, and half the bread crumbs. Mix very well. Prepare the bechamel sauce. (See in sauces, bechamel regular). Put half the potatoes in a baking pan, one next to the other. Cover them with the ground meat and over it put the remaining potatoes. Over the potatoes, put the bechamel sauce. Pour the remaining cheese and bread crumbs, sprinkl with the 4 table spoons melted butter and bake in medium oven for 40 minutes. Let it cool and serve.

Wash the eggplants, and cut them in thin slices. Put salt and pepper. Heat the olive oil in a frying pan and fry them. In a saucepan put olive oil, onion, groung meat, tomatoes, parsley, salt, and pepper, and saute, for 10 minutes. Add the wine and cook for 5 minutes. Add 1 cup water, cover the saucepan and cook for half an hour, until the liquid has been absorbed. Remove from the fire, add half the cheese and half the bread crumbs. Mix very well. Prepare the bechamel sauce. (See in sauces, bechamel sauce regular). Butter a medium size baking pan, and put half the eggplants in, one next to the other. Cover them with the ground meat, and over it the rest of the eggplants. Cover them with the bechamel sauce. Pour on the sauce the remaining cheese and bread crumbs, sprinkle with the 4 table spoons melted butter. Bake in medium oven for 40 minutes. Let it cool and serve.

MEATS

Meats are the most significant and tasteful food. The meats separate to: beef, lamb, pork, game, and poultry. There are many ways to cook meat: Boiled, oily, roast, grill, or fried.

For the boiled meats:

The meat must boil with cold water, not to loose its taste and flow its liquid: Skim, because the foam is dirty and must come off, because it coagulate under in the proportion temperature and stay on the meat. In boil meat the most taste is in the liquid.

For roast meats:

They have excellent taste, because they keep their liquids. The outside forms a crust, which does not let the meat juice to escape which would dry the meat. Before putting it in the oven, rub it with lemon and lightly coat with flour or bread crumbs.

For grilled meats:

Must be cooked in strong fire, and during cooking sprinkle with olive oil and lemon sauce.

For oily meats:

Roast brown with olive oil and onion or hot melted butter. Always cooked with spices or aromatic herbs, which gives them a nice taste, and savory sauce. One must not brown roast for a long time because they burn. Instead they must be a light brown colour. When finish cooking the meat, one must add wine or lemon, adding it little by little to make steam, so it will help the juice come out of the meat.

When you buy meat, be careful not to have:

a) many thick fat fibrils
b) a dark colour
c) a dark red colour mixed with light red
d) very fresh and bloody in fibrils
e) yellowish liquids or
f) yellow colour to the bones

Meats are dividend in three categories:

The red meat, that is: beef, horse, lamb, veal, pork.

The white meat, that is: rabbit, poultry.

The black meat, that is: all the game and wild boar.

After the animal is slain, it must stay 36 hours in the refrigerator, before being consumed, except the intestines which must consumed when fresh.

BOILED MEAT VRASTO KREAS

BEEF OR VEAL BOILED VODINO E MOSHARI VRASTO

Preparation time 120 minutes For 8 persons

1 1/2 kilo (3 lb, or 54 OZ) beef or veal meat bosom
1 cup rice or that pastry you like
3 stalks celery
1/2 kilo (1 lb, or 18 OZ) potatoes
1/2 kilo (1 lb, or 18 OZ) ripe tomatoes
4 carrots
2 medium onions
5 squash, salt

BOILED PORK THIGH

HIRINO BOUTI VRASTO

Preparation time 180 minutes For 8 persons

1 1/2 kilo (3 lb, or 54 OZ) pork thigh
1 garlic bulb
3 bay leaves, salt, pepper

LAMBS' FEET WITH WHITE SAUCE

PODARAKIA ARNISIA ME ASPRI SALTSA

Preparation time 120 minutes For 6 persons

12 lambs' feet
2 medium onions
3 stalks celery
3 carrots
4 table spoons butter
3 table spoons flour
2 egg yolks
1 lemon, salt, pepper
1 table spoon chopped parsley
2 cups meat broth

Wash the meat and put it with very salted water to boil. Skim and let it boil for half an hour. Clean and wash the vegetables. Do not cut them. Put them in, with the boiling meat and boil 30 more minutes. Remove from the fire and drain in very thin strainer. Put the broth back on the fire, add some more water if is necessary and continue to boil. Ground the tomatoes and put their pulp in the boiling broth. Add rice (after the broth has boiled), mix and let it boil for another 20 minutes. Cut the meat in slices and garnish it with the vegetables. Keeping them warm. Serve with the warm broth.

Wash the meat very good. Pierce meat with a large tined fork. Make some holes on it and place a piece of garlic in each hole. Salt the meat and put it in a saucepan with very much water, and with the bay leaves. Skim and boil for two and half hours. Drain it and let cool. Cut it in slices and serve cold with potatoes or pilaf or macaroni, which you will boil in its broth. Or just serve with salad.

Clean and wash the feet very well and spread open the trotters. Using with alcohol sing the feet very well.

Wash them in hot water and put them in a saucepan with salted water to cover them. Add to the water onions, celery and carrots.

When the vegetables and the meat boil, drain them and keep the vegetables aside. Debone the feet and cut each of them in 3 pieces. Keep them warm. In a sauce pan put the butter to melt. Add flour mixing continuously until dissolved. Add the 2 cups meat broth, salt, pepper, and mix to thicken the sauce. Beat the eggs with the lemon juice and add them to the sauce. Pour the sauce over the lambs' feet, over the sauce, put the parsley and garnish with carrots. Serve warm 2 feet to each person.

PIHTI

PIHTI

Preparation time 240 minutes More than 12 persons

1 pig's head
10 pepper corns
4 carrots
4 stalks celery
10 cloves garlic
5 bay leaves
4 table spoons vinegar
1/2 table spoon cumin
1/2 table spoon pepper powder
1/2 table spoon salt

LAMB FRICASSE

ARNI FRICASSE

Preparation time 120 minutes For 8 persons

2 kilos (4 lb, or 72 OZ) lamb thigh
1/2 cup butter
2 small heads of lettuce
2 onions
2 carrots
2 stalks dill
2 stalks celery
2 lemons
2 eggs
3 table spoons flour
salt, pepper, water as needed

Wash the head very well in warm water to drain the blood and clean it well. Boil it with plenty of salted water and the pepper corns. Skim and let it boil for half an hour. Add the carrots, celery, onions, garlic and bay leaves. Continue boiling for half an hour or more if needed. Drain and let the head cool. Open it and cut its meat in small pieces. Keep the broth. Drain the broth and add the vinegar.

Put the meat in an oblong form and lay it uniform. Add the broth to the meat but mix it first with the cumin and the pepper. When it cools, put the pihti in the refrigerator to thicken. Serve it cool.   93

Cut the meat in parts, wash it very well and put it in a saucepan with 3 cups salted water. Bring to a boil. In the mean time clean and wash the vegetables. Cut them in small pieces. Add them to the meat, adding 3 more cups water and let them boil.

Remove from the fire and drain. Measure 3 cups liquid. Put the butter in a saucepan to melt. Add the flour little by little mixing continously to dissolve. Add the food's broth and the lemon juice. Mix continously to thicken the sauce. Add salt and pepper, the 2 egg yolks, some water, mix and put this sauce in the meat. Shake the saucepan with your hands to spread the sauce and serve the food warm.

MEAT WITH VEGETABLES AND OLIVE OIL

KREAS ME LAHANIKA KE LADI

LAMB WITH ARTICHOKES AND EGG AND LEMON SAUC

ARNI ME AGINARES AVGOLEMONO

Preparation time 120 minutes For 6 persons

1 1/2 kilo (3 lb, or 54 OZ) lamb
1 1/2 cup olive oil
6 large artichokes
3 fresh chopped scallions
1 table spoon chopped dill
2 lemons, 2 eggs
salt, pepper, water as needed

LAMB WITH SQUASH AND TOMATO

ARNI ME KOLOKITHAKIA KE DOMATA

Preparation time 90 minutes For 6 persons
1 1/2 kilo (3 lb, or 54 OZ) lamb breast
1 1/2 cup olive oil
1 large chopped onion
1 1/2 kilo (3 lb, or 54 OZ) squash
1/2 kilo (1 lb, or 18 OZ) ground ripe tomatoes
salt, pepper, water as needed

LAMB OR VEAL WITH POTATOES

ARNI E MOSHARI ME PATATES

Preparation time 160 minutes For 6 persons

1 1/2 kilo (3 lb, or 54 OZ) lamb or beef thigh
1 1/2 cup olive oil
1 lemon, salt, pepper
1 kilo (2 lb, or 36 OZ) potatoes
3 cups olive oil for frying

Cut the meat in parts and wash it well. Put it in a saucepan with the olive oil and the onions and saute. Add the dill, salt, pepper, mix and let stand for 5 minutes. Add 2 cups water and cook in medium fire for half an hour. Clean the artichokes of their leaves. Cut them in two and remove their fluff. Rub them with lemon and put them in water with lemon juice in. When finished wash them off and add to the saucepan. Add half the lemon juice, mix and cook for 15 to 20 minutes, until the food be with its liquid. Remove from the fire. Beat the eggs add the remaining lemon juice to the eggs and the liquid from the food. Mix very well and pour the sauce over the meat. Shake the saucepan with your hands to spread the sauce, and put again on very low fire for 5 minutes. Serve warm.

Cut the meat in parts and wash it very well. In a saucepan put, the meat, onion, tomatoes, salt and pepper and saute. Add 1 cup water and cook over low fire for 40 minutes. Wash the squash and cut them in 3 round pieces. Add them to the meat. Add 1 more cup water and cook for 20 more minutes. Remove from the fire and serve the food warm.

Wash the meat very well. In a saucepan put the olive oil with the salted meat and the lemon juice. Let it cook for 10 minutes. Add 2 cups hot water and cook in low fire for 40 minutes, adding water sometimes if is needed. When it is cooked, drain and cool. Cut it in thin slices.

Clean and wash the potatoes. Cut them in round slices and salt. Heat the olive oil in a frying pan and fry the potatoes. Do not fry them completely. Put them in the saucepan which you have cooked the meat. Add to the meat sauce 1 cup hot water and cook for 10 minutes. Lay the potatoes and the meat slices, and cook for 7 more minutes. Serve the food warm.

LAMB OR VEAL WITH PEA

ARNI E MOSHARI ME ARAKA

Preparation time 90 minutes For 6 persons

1 1/2 kilo (3 lb, or 54 OZ) lamb or veal
1 1/2 cup butter
1 1/2 kilo (3 lb, or 54 OZ) frozen peas
1/2 kilo (1 lb, or 18 OZ) ground ripe tomatoes
1 large chopped onion
1 table spoon chopped parsley fresh
1 table spoon chopped dill fresh
salt - pepper - water as needed

LAMB OR VEAL WITH VEGETABLES

ARNI E MOSHARI ME LAHANIKA

Preparation time 225 minutes For 6 persons

1 1/2 kilo (3 lb, or 54 OZ) lamb or veal
2 1/2 cups olive oil
5 fresh chopped scallions
1/2 kilo (1 lb, or 18 OZ) potatoes
1/2 kilo (1 lb, or 18 OZ) squash
1/2 kilo (1 lb, or 18 OZ) peas
5 carrots
2 table spoons chopped parsley fresh
1/2 kilo (1 lb, or 18 OZ) ground ripe tomatoes
salt, pepper

LAMB WITH STRING BEANS

ARNI ME FASOLAKIA FRESKA

Preparation time 120 minutes For 4 persons

1 kilo (2 lb, or 36 OZ) lamb (part of the back)
1 kilo (2 lb, or 36 OZ) string beans
1 1/2 cup olive oil
1 large chopped onion
1/2 kilo (1 lb, or 18 OZ) ground ripe tomatoes
2 stalks fresh chopped parsley
salt, pepper

Cut the meat in parts and wash it very well. Put it in a saucepan with the butter, onion, tomatoes, dill, parsley, salt, pepper and saute for 10 minutes. Add 2 cups water and cook over low fire for 45 minutes. Add peas, 1 cup water and cook for 15 more minutes. When peas and meat are cooked, remove from the fire. Serve the food warm.

Clean and wash the vegetables. Cut each potato into four pieces, the carrots and the squash in round slices. Salt them. Wash and cut the meat in parts. Salt and pepper it. In a frying pan heat the olive oil and half-fry the meat in low fire unitl golden brown. Do not burn it. When finish with the meat, in the same oil fry the potatoes, carrots, squash and onions not to cook at all.

Put the olive oil from the frying pan into a baking pan. Add the meat, and the vegetables. Add the parsley, and pour the ground tomatoes over the food. Add 2 cups water and bake in medium oven for 2 hours. Serve warm.

Clean the string beans and wash them. Cut the meat in parts, wash and put them in saucepan. Add the olive oil, onions, tomatoes and saute for 15 minutes. Add the string beans, parsley, salt, pepper, 1 cup water and cook over low fire for 30 minutes. If the food needs more water add some. Serve warm.

LAMB WITH SQUASH AND EGG AND LEMON SAUCE

ARNI ME KOLOKITHAKIA KE SALTSA AVGOLEMONO

Preparation time 90 minutes For 4 persons

1 kilo (2 lb, or 36 OZ) lamb's breast
1 kilo (2 lb, or 36 OZ) squash
1 1/2 cup butter
4 fresh chopped scallions
1 table spoon chopped dill
2 lemons, 2 eggs, salt, pepper

LAMB OR VEAL STEW

MOSHARI E ARNI STIFADO

Preparation time 150 minutes For 6 persons

1 1/2 kilo (3 lb, or 54 OZ) lamb or veal meat without bones
1 1/2 cup olive oil
1/2 kilo (1 lb, or 18 OZ) ground ripe tomatoes
1 1/2 kilo (3 lb, or 54 OZ) onions
10 cloves of garlic
1/2 cup wine
2 table spoons chopped parsley
salt, pepper, 4 bay leaves

LAMB OR VEAL WITH OKRA

ARNI E MOSHARI ME BAMIES

Preparation time 120 minutes For 4 persons

1 kilo (2 lb, or 36 OZ) lamb or veal thigh meat
1 kilo (2 lb, or 36 OZ) okra
1/2 kilo (1 lb, or 18 OZ) ground ripe tomatoes
1 large chopped onion
1 1/2 cup olive oil
2 lemons, salt, pepper

Cut the meat in parts and wash it good. In a saucepan put, the butter, meat, onions and saute for 10 minutes. Add 1 cup water and cook for 30 minutes. Clean and wash the squash. Cut them in round pieces.

Add them to the meat. Add the dill, salt and pepper. Add 1 cup water and cook for 20 more minutes. Remove of the fire. Beat the eggs with some water and lemons juice, to mix well. Take some liquid from the food and add it into the eggs. Beat well and pour with the sauce over the food. Put the saucepan back on the fire and cook with very low fire for 10 minutes. Serve warm.

Cut the meat in small pieces. Wash it good. Clean the onions and cut them in thick slices. In a saucepan put the olive oil, the meat, and the onions and saute for 15 minutes. Add the wine, tomatoes, parsley, bay leaves, garlic, salt, pepper and cook over low fire for 90 minutes. Add warm water if it is needed during cooking. Serve warm with pilaf or fried potatoes.

Wash and clean the okra, cutting their tops off. Salt and put them in a baking pan with the lemon. Wash the meat and cut it in parts. In a saucepan put the olive oil, onion, and the meat, and saute for 15 minutes. Add the ground tomatoes, 2 cups water and cook for 15 more minutes. Add the okra, salt, pepper, and cook over low fire for 20 minutes. Serve warm.

VEAL OR BEEF WITH SPINACH AND EGG AND LEMON SAUCE

MOSHARI E VODINO ME SPANAKI AVGOLEMONO

Preparation time 180 minutes For 6 persons

1 1/2 kilo (3 lb, or 54 OZ) veal or beef
1 1/2 kilo (3 lb, or 54 OZ) spinach
1 1/2 cup olive oil
1 large chopped onion
2 lemons, 2 eggs, salt and pepper

PORK WITH CELERY AND EGG AND LEMON SAUCE

HIRINO ME SELINO KE SALTSA AVGOLEMONO

Preparation time 120 minutes For 6 persons

1 1/2 kilo (3 lb, or 54 OZ) pork meat
1 cup olive oil
2 kilos (4 lb, or 72 OZ) celery
2 chopped onions
2 lemons, 2 eggs, salt, pepper
1 table spoon conr-flour

PORK WITH CABBAGE

HIRINO ME LAHANO

Preparation time 180 minutes For 6 persons

1 1/2 kilo (3 lb, or 54 OZ) pork meat
2 kilos (4 lb, or 72 OZ) cabbage
1 1/2 cup olive oil
1/2 kilo (1 lb, or 18 OZ) ground ripe tomatoes
2 large chopped onions
5 cloves garlic
3 stalks chopped celery
3 bay leaves
1/2 cup grated cheese, salt, pepper

Cut the meat in parts and wash it good. In a saucepan put the olive oil, meat, onion and saute for 10 minutes. Add 2 cups water and cook over low fire for 1 hour. Clean the spinach, cut it in 3 pieces and wash it. Put it in salted boiling water to boil for 10 minutes. Drain it. Add spinach to the meat, add salt, pepper, 2 cups water and cook over low fire for 1 more hour. Remove from the fire. Beat the eggs with the lemon. Add liquid of the food to the eggs and beat very well. Pour this sauce over the meat, put back on the fire for 5 minutes more and serve warm.

Clean the celery, wash and cut it in 3 pieces. In a saucepan boil salted water and add the celery, bring to a half boil. Drain. Cut the meat in parts, wash, salt and pepper it. In a saucepan put, the meat the olive oil, onions and saute for 10 minutes. Add 3 cups water and cook over low fire for half an hour. Add the celery and cook for 15 to 20 minutes more. Dissolve the corn flour in 1/2 cup water. Beat the eggs with the lemon and add the corn flour in. Add liquid from the food, beat all these to mix well and pour the sauce over the food. Shake the saucepan with your hands to spread the sauce, put back on the fire for 5 more minutes and serve the food warm.

Open the cabbage and wash it. Put it in salted boiling water and bring to a half-boil. Drain it. Wash the meat and cut it in parts.

In a saucepan put the garlic, celery, meat, 1 cup water and cook for 15 minutes. Add the olive oil and cook for 5 minutes. Add the tomatoes, bay leaves, salt, pepper and cook over low fire for 90 minutes. Add the cabbage cut in slices and cook for 20 more minutes. Serve the food warm with the grated cheese on top.

BAKED-FRIED-GRILLED MEAT PSITO-TIGANITO-SHAR KREAS

THIGH LAMB STUFFED ARNISIO BOUTI GEMISTO

Preparation time 160 minutes For 6 to 8 persons

1 1/2 kilo (3 lb, or 54 OZ) lamb thigh without the bone
1 cup butter
1 1/2 kilo (3 lb, or 54 OZ) small potatoes
1 cup wine
3 table spoons chopped parsley
salt and pepper

VEAL OR LAMB WITH POTATOES IN THE OVEN

MOSHARI E ARNI ME PATATES STO FOURNO

Preparation time 120 minutes For 4 persons

1 kilo (2 lb, or 36 OZ) lamb or veal
1 kilo (2 lb, or 36 OZ) small potatoes
1 cup butter
2 lemons, some flour, salt, pepper

BAKED LAMB WITH SQUASH

ARNI ME KOLOKITHAKIA STO FOURNO

Preparation time 120 minutes For 4 persons

1 kilo (2 lb, or 36 OZ) lamb thigh
1 cup butter
1 kilo (2 lb, or 36 OZ) squash
1/2 kilo (1 lb, or 18 OZ) ripe tomatoes
salt, pepper

Pound the meat to tenderize. Wash and rub it with salt, pepper and parsley. Wrap it up with a string. Put it in a baking pan with the butter and put it in a very hot oven to golden brown all the sides. Add the wine, 2 cups water. Baste the meat with juice and bake for half an hour. Clean the potatoes, wash and salt them. Do not cut them if they are small. Add them to the baking pan. Add 2 more cups water, baste the meat again with its liquid. Bake in medium oven for 90 minutes. Remove from the oven, allow to cool and cut it in slices. Serve.

Wash the meat very well. Rub it with salt, pepper, half the lemon and coat with flour. Put it in a baking pan. Peel the potatoes and use them whole if they are small. Put them around the meat. Add the melted butter, the rest of the lemon juice, 2 cups water and bake in medium oven for 90 minutes. Serve warm.

Note: Roast the pork the same way.

Wash the meat. Salt and pepper it. Wash the tomatoes and cut them in very small slieces. Wash the squash. Cut them in 3 pieces. Salt and pepper all of them. In a baking pan put the tomato slices and over them lay the meat. Add the melted butter and bake in medium oven for half an hour. Add the squash and bake for 45 minutes more. Serve warm.

BAKED LAMB OR VEAL WITH PASTE

ARNI E MOSHARI ME KRITHARAKI STO FOURNO

Preparation time 135 minutes For 6 persons

1 1/2 kilo (3 lb, or 54 OZ) lamb or veal
1/2 kilo (1 lb, or 18 OZ) barley paste
1 cup butter
1/2 kilo (1 lb, or 18 OZ) ground ripe tomatoes
1 cup grated cheese, salt, pepper

VEAL WITH TOMATOES

MOSHARI KOKKINISTO

Preparation time 145 minutes For 6 persons

1 1/2 kilo (3 lb, or 54 OZ) veal
1/2 kilo (1 lb, or 18 OZ) ground ripe tomatoes
1 1/2 cup olive oil, salt, pepper

MIXED GRILL

SOUVLAKIA ANAMIKTA

Preparation time 90 minutes For 6 persons

250gr. (1/2 lb, or 9 OZ) beef
250gr. (1/2 lb, or 9 OZ) pork
250gr. (1/2 lb, or 9 OZ) lamb
salt, pepper, cumin, oregano

Wash the meat. Grind the tomatoes. Put the meat in a baking pan add salt and pepper. Add the melted butter and the tomatoes. Put the food in medium oven and baked for 45 minutes. Add 5 cups water and when it will boil add the barley paste and bake for 30 minutes. Take the food out of the oven when is done. Serve warm with the meat cut in slices. Sprinkle with grated cheese and serve with salad.

Cut the meat in parts and wash it. Put it in a saucepan with the olive oil, tomatoes, and 2 cups warm water, salt, pepper and cook over low fire for 2 hours. When it will be with its liquid, remove from the fire. Serve warm with fried potatoes, or pilaf, or macaroni, or squash or fried eggplants.

Wash the meat very well, cut them in small cubes, salt and pepper them, and coat with cumin and oregano. Put the meat cubes on skewers like this: 1 piece beef, 1 piece pork, 1 piece lamb, continue this until finish with all meat cubes. On each skewer do not put more than 6 pieces if skewer is small. Heat the grill and lay on, the souvlakia which you have pour with olive oil, and turn skewers to cook meat on all sides. Serve warm, with season's salad, or pilaf, or fried potatoes.

Note: The souvlakia can be made with only beef, pork or lamb. You can also use the liver or the kidney of the meat you prefer.

SOUVLAKIA WITH MEAT AND VEGETABLES

SOUVLAKIA ME KREAS KE LAHANIKA

Preparation time 90 minutes For 6 persons

1 kilo (2 lb, or 36 OZ) thigh of lamb
4 ripe tomatoes
4 medium onions
4 green bell-peppers, salt, pepper

VEAL LOAF

MOSHARI ROLO

Preparation time 145 minutes For 8 persons

1 1/2 kilo (3 lb, or 54 OZ) boneless shoulder
1 1/2 kilo (3 lb, or 54 OZ) ground ripe tomatoes
1 cup butter
1 cup white wine
1/2 cup chopped parsley
5 cloves garlic, salt, pepper
250gr. (1/2 lb, or 9 OZ) feta cheese

FRIED STEAKS

BRIZOLES STO TIGANI

Preaparation time 45 minutes

GRILLED STEAKS

BRIZOLES STI SHARA

Preparation time 45 minutes

Wash the meat and cut it in small cubes. Wash the vegetables and cut them in thick slices. Salt and pepper, meat and vegetables. Put on skewers 1 piece onion, 1 piece meat, 1 piece tomato, 1 piece meat, 1 piece green pepper, 1 piece meat, 1 piece onion.

Continue this until all the ingredients are finish. Pour with olive oil and put the souvlakia on very hot grill. The fire which cook the souvlakia must be always low. Cook the souvlakia and serve warm with pilaf, or fried potatoes or season salad.

Note: The meat can be beef or pork too.

Open the meat in two. Wash it. Pepper and salt it. Put inside it, the garlic, parsley and feta cheese cut in thin slices. Fold the meat and shape into a roll. Tie it with a piece of string. In a large sauce pan melt the butter and brown the meat on all sides. Add the tomatoes, 2 cups warm water and cook over low fire for 1 hour. Let it cool and cut it in slices. Serve with fried potatoes, or baked potatoes, or pilaf or macaroni.

Pound the steaks to tenderize. Wash, salt and pepper them. Put them in a frying pan to cook with some water. When water evaporates, add some olive oil and let them cook until golden brown. Add the juice of 1 lemon or 1/2 cup wine, and let cook for 5 minutes. Serve warm, with fried potatoes, or boiled vegetables or season salad. Steaks can be beef, pork or lamb (chops).

Pound the steaks to tenderize and wash them. Put salt, pepper some oregano and lay on very hot grill. Cook over low fire. During cooking sprinkle with olive oil and lemon sauce (see sauces). Cook both sides. Serve warm with boiled vegetables, or fried potatoes or season's salad. The steaks could be beef, pork or lamb (chops).

MEAT BALLS GRILLED

KEFTEDES STI SHARA

Preparation time 45 minutes For 4 persons

750gr. (1 3/4 lb, or 27 OZ) chopped meat
1/2 cup bread crumbs
2 eggs, 1 table spoon melted butter
salt, pepper, some mint

BEEF TONGUE WITH TOMATO SAUCE

GLOSSA VODINI ME SALTSA DOMATAS

Preparation time 180 minutes For 8 persons

1 beef tongue
2 onions
4 carrots
6 stalks selery
750gr (1 3/4 lb, or 27 OZ) ground ripe tomatoes
1 cup butter
1/2 cup white wine
1 piece cinnamon
5 cloves
salt, pepper, broth from the boiled tongue

SAUSAGES AND INTESTINES

LOUKANIKA KE ENTOSTHIA KOKORETSI

Preparation time 240 minutes

2 lambs liver
1 lung of lamb
2 hearts of lamb
2 spleens of lamb
intestine coverings of the lamb
kidneys, salt, pepper, oregano, olive oil

Put in a bowl the chopped meat. Add the bread crumbs, eggs, melted butter, salt, pepper and mint. Mix very well. Heat the grill, apply oil on it and cook over low fire, both sides. Serve warm with salad, or pilaf, or fried potatoes or mashed potatoes.

Scrape the tongue with a knife very well. Wash it in plenty of water and boil it in salted water for 15 minutes.

Drain it. Discard water. Put fresh warm water in a saucepan, put the tongue in, 1 onion cut in two, 2 carrots cut in half, 3 stalks celery cut in half, some salt, and boil for 2 hours until the tongue will be very soft. Drain and keep the broth. Put the tongue in, cold water. Take off the rough skin with a knife and the two bones at the base of the tongue. Melt the butter in a saucepan. Put the tongue in and saute on all sides, add the other onion chopped, carrots and celery chopped. Saute. Add salt, pepper, wine and cook for 5 minutes. Then add the ground tomatoes, 2 cups of the tongue broth, cinnamon, cloves, and cook over low fire, for 40 minutes. Remove from the fire and cut it in slices. Serve warm with its sauce and fried potatoes or pilaf.

Note: Remove cinnamon and the cloves from the sauce, before serving.

Turn the intestines inside out and wash them very well with hot water. Turn back on the right side. Cut the meats in big pieces and wash them very well.

Put salt, pepper, oregano and put them on a spit (a big one). Put: Liver, spleen, heard, lung, sweetbread and continue like this until all the meat are put on the spit. Pin the intestine side at the spit and cover with it the meat, in closesly distance. When 1 intestine finish continue by tieing a second one with the preceding and continue wraping up.

Season the kokoretsi put pepper and oregano and sprinkle with olive oil. Spit on low fire for 2 to 2 1/2 hours. Serve warm, with other meat and salads, cut in slices.

MEAT BALLS WITH EGG AND LEMON SAUCE

GIOUVARLAKIA AVGOLEMONO

Preparation time 90 minutes For 8 persosn

750gr. (1 3/4 lb, or 27 OZ) ground meat
1/2 cup butter
1/2 cup rice
1 chopped onion
1/2 cup chopped parsley
2 eggs, 2 lemons
salt, pepper, water as needed

SAUSAGE WITH GROUND MEAT

SOUTZOUKAKIA ME KIMA

Preparation time 90 minutes For 6 persons

750gr (1 3/4 lb, or 27 OZ) ground meat
1/2 kilo (1 lb, or 18 OZ) ground ripe tomatoes
1 chopped onion
1/2 cup bread crumbs
1 tea spoon cumin
2 1/2 cups olive oil for frying
salt, pepper

Put the ground meat in a bowl. Add the toast bread crumbs the cumin, salt, pepper and mix well. Mold into oblong cylinders, 9 centimeter long. Fry them on all sides in very hot olive oil. When finish frying, add in the same olive oil the ground tomatoes, the onion and saute for 5 minutes. Add the soutzoukakia in, and fry over low fire for 15 minutes. Serve warm with fried potatoes, or macaroni or pilaf.

Wash the rice well. Put the ground meat in a bowl and add in: rice, parsley, onion, egg whites, salt, pepper and mix well. Make round meat balls as big as a walnut. Put in a saucepan the butter to melt. Add the meat-balls, warm water as much as needed to cover. Boil over low fire until 2 cups liquid remains.

Beat the egg yolks with the lemons. Add the liquid of the food and beat well. Pour the sauce over meat-balls and cook with low fire for 5 minutes. Mix sauce and other ingredients and serve the food warm.

POULTRY AND GAME

CHICKEN FILAF

KOTOPOULO PILAFI

Preparation time 120 minutes For 6 persons

1 large chicken (2 kilos, or 4 lb, or 72 OZ) approximately
1 cup olive oil
1/2 kilo (1 lb or 18 OZ) rice
1/2 kilo (1 lb or 18 OZ) ground ripe tomatoes
1 chopped onion, salt, pepper

RABBIT OR HARE STEW

KOUNELI E LAGOS STIFADO

Preparation time 180 minutes For 8 persons

1 rabbit or 1 hare about 2 kilos (4 lb or 72 OZ)
2 cups olive oil
1 kilo (2 lb, or 36 OZ) ground ripe tomatoes
1 1/2 kilo (3 lb, or 54 OZ) small onions
1 garlic bulb
5 bay leaves
1 cup vinegar
salt, pepper corns

CHICKEN WITH PEAS

KOTOPOULO ME ARAKA

Preparation time 110 minutes For 4 persons

1 chicken 1 kilo (2 lb, or 36 OZ)
1 cup olive oil
750gr. (1 3/4 lb, or 27 OZ) ground ripe tomatoes
1 kilo peas (2 lb, or 36 OZ)
1 chopped onion
salt, pepper, water as needed

Cut the chicken into 6 parts. Wash very well. In a saucepan put the olive oil. Add the chicken in, onion and tomatoes. Saute for 10 minutes. Salt and pepper. Add 2 cups hot water and cook for 20 minutes. Add 5 cups water and let it boil for 20 more minutes. Drain the meat and put the liquid back in the saucepan. As soon as it will boil add the washed rice and let it cook. Mix with a fork. When is done serve it warm with the chicken.

Note: The chicken can be cooked with or without rice. You can serve with fried potatoes or macaroni and season salad.

Cut the meat in parts and wash it. Put it in a baking pan with the vinegar for 20 minutes. In the mean time clean the onions but do not cut them. Ground the tomatoes. In a saucepan put the olive oil with the meat. Add the onions, tomatoes, garlic, bay leaves, salt and pepper, mix very well and saute for 20 minutes. Add 2 cups hot water, cover the saucepan and cook over low fire for 90 minutes. Add more water if need it. When the meat is cooked remove from the fire. Serve the food warm with fried potatoes.

Wash and clean the chicken. Cut it in 4 parts. Ground the tomatoes. In a saucepan put the olive oil, onion, tomatoes and chicken, salt and pepper and saute for 20 minutes. Add 2 cups water and cook in low fire for 45 minutes, with the saucepan cover. Add the pea, cook for 20 more minutes and remove of the fire. Serve them with season's salad, and fried potatoes.

157

RABBIT OR HARE WITH TOMATO SAUCE

KOUNELI E LAGOS ME SALTSA DOMATA

Preparation time 120 minutes For 8 persons

Rabbit or hare about 2 kilos (4lb, or 72 OZ)
2 cups olive oil
1 garlic bulb
1 cup white wine
1 kilo (2 lb, or 36 OZ) ground ripe tomatoes
salt and pepper

CHICKEN WITH TOMATO SAUCE

KOTOPOULO KOKINISTO

Preparation time 160 minutes For 4 persons

1 chicken not very big about (3 lb, or 54 OZ)
1/2 kilo (1 lb, or 18 OZ) ground ripe tomatoes
1 cup olive oil
1/2 cup wine
1 stick cinnamon
5 cloves
salt, pepper, water as needed

DUCK WITH OKRA

PAPIA ME BAMIES

Preparation time 240 minutes For 6 persons

3 small duck
2 cups olive oil
1 kilo (2 lb, or 36 OZ) ripe tomatoes
1 kilo (2 lb, or 36 OZ) okra
1/2 cup white wine
1 chopped onion
3 lemons, salt, pepper

Wash the meat and cut it in parts. Salt and pepper it. Heat the olive oil in a frying pan and fry the meat. When finished in the same olive oil add the garlic, tomatoes and the wine and saute for 20 minutes. Put the fried meat in a saucepan and pour over it, the tomato sauce. Add 2 cups hot water and cook in low fire for half an hour. Serve warm with fried potatoes or pilaf and season's salad.

Clean and wash the chicken. Cut it in parts. Put the olive oil in a saucepan and the chicken and saute it on all sides. Add the wine let cook for 5 minutes and add the tomatoes, cinnamon, cloves, salt, pepper and cook in low fire. Add occasionally some hot water and cook for 90 minutes. Remove from the fire and serve with fried potatoes or mashed potatoes or pilaf or macaroni and season's salad.

Clean the duck very well and sew them. Clean and wash the okra. Put them in a baking pan with the lemon juice and let them. Half of the tomatoes grind them, and the rest just peel them.

Put the half olive oil in a saucepan to heat and lightly brown the duck. Add the onion, wine and let for 5 minutes. Add the ground tomatoes. Salt, pepper, add 1 cup water (hot) and cook over low fire for 1 hour. With the rest of the olive oil fry the okra. Lay them in a baking pan, with the peeled tomatoes. Add salt and pepper and the sauce in which the ducks are cooked. Bake in medium oven for 1 hour. Cut the ducks in half and put them on the okra, 20 minutes before you take out of the oven. Serve warm.

FISH AND SEA FOOD

FISH SOUVLAKIA

SOUVLAKIA PSARIOU

Preparation time 120 minutes For 4 persons

1 1/2 kilo (3 lb, or 54 OZ) swordfish
1/2 kilo (1 lb, or 18 OZ) shrimps
1 1/2 cup olive oil
2 lemons, 4 tomatoes
4 green bell peppers
1 small can mushrooms, salt

FRIED DRIED CODFISH

BAKALIAROS PASTOS TIGANITOS

Preparation time 60 minutes For 6 persons

2 kilos (4lb, or 72 OZ) dried codfish
1/2 kilo (1 lb, or 18 OZ) flour
2 eggs
1 tea spoon baking powder
3 cups olive oil
1 garlic bulb

DRIED CODFISH WITH POTATOES AND TOMATO SAUC

BAKALIAROS PASTOS ME PATATES KE SALTSA DOMATAS

Preparation time 120 minutes For 6 persons

1 1/2 kilo (3 lb, or 54 OZ) dried codfish
1 kilo (2 lb, or 36 OZ) potatoes
1 1/2 cup olive oil
1 kilo (2 lb, or 36 OZ) ground ripe tomatoes
1 chopped onion
10 garlic cloves, salt, pepper

Clean the swordfish of its skin. Wash it well and cut it in not very small pieces. Wash the shrimps and boil them. Shell them. Cut the tomatoes, green bell pepper and mushrooms in slices. Salt the fish and vegetables. Take a skewer and pin one piece of bell pepper, 1 piece of sword fish, one or two shrimps, 1 piece of mushroom.

Note: If the mushrooms are small use them whole. Place all pieces on skewers. Mix the olive oil with the lemon juice and coat souvlakia. Apply oil to the grill and grill the souvlakia in low fire turning to cook all sides. Serve them warm with oil and lemon sauce and season's salad. Serve about 3 souvlakia to each person.

Wash the codfish to remove most of the salt and put it in a bowl with water for 10 hours to remove the salt. Change the water 3-4 times. Cut fish in big pieces and remove its skin, and bones. Mix the flour with baking powder and dissolve it in 3 cups (about) water. Beat the eggs and add them into the flour. Must make a thick batter. Heat the olive oil. Put each piece of codfish in the batter and put it in the frying pan to fry until golden brown on all sides. Finish frying and serve the codfish warm, with garlic sauce. Prepare the garlic sauce (see in sauces). Serve also with beet-roots or boiled vegetables.

Put the codfish in the water for 10 hours to remove the salt. Remove its skin and the bones and cut it in parts. Clean the potatoes, wash and cut each one in four pieces. Clean the garlic, and grind the tomatoes. Chop the onion. In a saucepan put, the olive oil with onion to saute. Add the tomatoes, and garlic and cook for 5 minutes. Add the potatoes, 1 cup water and cook over low fire for 30 minutes. Add the codfish, 2 cups water and cook over low fire for 30 more minutes, until the food is with little sauce. Serve it warm.

FISH FILLET WITH WINE

PSARI GLOSA KRASATO

Preparation time 45 minutes For 4 persons

1 kilo filleted fish (2 lb, or 36 OZ)
1/2 cup olive oil
1/2 kilo (1 lb, or 18 OZ) ripe tomatoes
1 onion
200gr. (1/2 lb, or 7 OZ) wine
1 table spoon chopped parsley
2 lemons, salt and pepper

GRILLED FISH

PSARI SHARAS

Preparation time 60 minutes For 4 persons

4 large fish whole
2 lemons
1 cup olive oil
1/2 cup chopped parsley

GREEK BOUILLABAISE

KAKAVIA

Preparation time 120 minutes For 6 persons

1 1/2 kilo (3 lb, or 54 OZ) miscellaneous fish
4 onions
4 carrots
4 stalks celery
4 tomatoes
1 cup olive oil
4 potatoes
4 squash
1/2 cup rice, salt, pepper

Clean the filleted fish and wash them well. Salt and pepper them. Put them in a baking pan with the olive oil, onion and tomatoes cut in slices. Pour the wine over and put them in warm oven for half an hour. Baste with their sauce while cooking. Remove from the oven and pour the lemon juice and the chopped parsley on top. Serve warm with boiled vegetables or season's salad.

Clean the fish of the scales and the intestines, washing them very well. Salt and pepper them. Heat the grill very much and lower the fire then. Oil the grill and place the fish on it. Grill both sides, adding oil sometimes. When grilled and light brown on both sides, mix the olive oil, and lemon juice and pour over the fish. Put the parsley on them and serve warm with season's salad.

Clean the fish and wash them well. Clean the vegetables and cut them in slices. In a saucepan put salted water and some pepper and put in the vegetables to boil for 10 minutes. Add the fish and boil all together about 45 to 60 minutes. Remove from the fire, drain and keep the broth. Clean the fish of their bones. Grind them. Grind the vegetables. Put the pulp of the fish, and the vegetables in a saucepan with the broth. Put it on the fire and add olive oil in. When starts to boil, add the washed rice. Mix and boil for 30 minutes. Serve the soup warm.

STUFFED SQUID

KALAMARAKIA GEMISTA

Preparation time 145 minutes For 6 persons

1 1/2 kilo (3 lb, or 54 OZ) squids
1 cup rice
2 cups olive oil
2 large chopped onions
1 cup chopped parsley
2 cups water
1 lemon, salt and pepper

PORGIES WITH CELERY AND EGG AND LEMON SAUCE

TSIPOURES ME SELINO KE SALTSA AVGOLEMONO

Preparation time 90 minutes For 4 persons

2 porgies about 2 kilos (4lb, or 72 OZ)
2 kilos (4lb, or 72 OZ) celery
1 cup olive oil
1 chopped onion
2 lemons, 2 eggs, salt and pepper

COOKED FISH PSARI

PLAKI STI KATSAROLA

Preparation time 90 minutes For 6 persons

1 1/2 kilo (3 lb, or 54 OZ) fish
1 1/2 cup olive oil
1 kilo (2 lb, or 36 OZ) ground ripe tomatoes
1/2 kilo (1 lb or 18 OZ) onions
1 garlic bulb
1 cup wine
1/2 cup chopped parsley, salt, pepper

Wash the squid very well. Remove the tresses and throw the ink sacks. Discard the fine bones and eyes. Remove the skin from the hoods, without cutting them. Chop the tresses. Wash all these very well. In a saucepan put the 1 cup olive oil with onions to saute. Add the tresses, parsley, salt, pepper, and 2 cups water and cook over low fire for 30 minutes. Add 2 more cups water and when it boils, wash the rice and add it in. Mix all together and cook for 15 minutes. When the stuffing thickens remove from the fire. Take each hood and with a teaspoon put some stuffing in. Sew it. Do like this with all hoods. Put them in a saucepan with the remaining olive oil, lemon juice and two cups water, and cook over low fire for 30 to 45 minutes. Serve warm with season's salad.

Clean and wash the porgies. Cut them in two. Clean the celery, cut each stalk in 3-4 pieces and wash it.

In a saucepan put the olive oil with the onion to saute. Add 2 cups water and when it boils add the celery, salt and pepper. Cook for 20 minutes. Add the fish, add some water if needed and cook for 30 minutes. Remove from the fire. Beat the eggs with the lemons. Add liquid from the food and beat well. Put the egg and lemon sauce in the fish and put the saucepan on low fire again for 5 minutes. Serve warm.

Clean and wash the fish very well. If the fish are small keep them whole. If it is big cut it in thick slices. Cut the onions in thin slices and chopp the garlic. Grind the tomatoes. In a saucepan put the olive oil and onions to saute. Add the wine little by little and let cook for 3 minutes. Add the tomatoes, parsley, garlic and cook for 5 more minutes. Salt and pepper. Add 1 cup water. Cook over low fire for 20 minutes. Add the fish. Cook over low fire for 30 minutes. Serve warm with fried potatoes and season's salad.

OCTOPUS WITH PILAF

HTAPODI PILAFI

Preparation time 120 minutes For 6 persons

1 1/2 kilo (3 lb, or 54 OZ) octopus
1 1/2 cup olive oil
1 1/2 cup rice
1 chopped onion, salt, pepper
1 kilo (2 lb, or 36 OZ) ground ripe tomatoes

LOBSTER WITH PILAF

ASTAKOS PILAFI

Preparation time 150 minutes For 6 persons

1 medium size lobster
1 1/2 cup olive oil
1 chopped onion
1 kilo (2 lb, or 36 OZ) ground ripe tomatoes
1 1/2 cup rice, salt, pepper

Wash the lobster very well. If the lobster is fresh tie its tail on its body with a piece of string. Put it in a saucepan and cover it with salted water. Boil for 40 minutes. Drain and keep the broth. Cool. Cut its legs, break them and remove the meat inside them. Cut its head, and its body on the back side of the head to the tail in two pieces. Remove all its meat and cut it in small pieces. Grind the tomatoes. Put in a saucepan the olive oil with the onion to saute. Add the tomatoes and after 5 minutes add the lobster's pieces. Add salt and pepper and cook for 15 minutes more. Drain the lobster's broth and take 2 cups. Add it to the saucepan. Wash the rice and as soon as the food boils, add the rice. Mix all very well and cook for 20 to 30 minutes, until the liquid has been absorbed. Cook over low fire. Remove from the fire and after 10 minutes serve the food warm.

Wash the octopus very well. Cut it in pieces and boil it with salted water for 1 hour. Drain and keep the broth. Put in a saucepan the olive oil with the onion and saute. Add the tomatoes and cook for 10 minutes.

Add the octopus and cook for 10 more minutes. As soon as the food boils, add 5 cups of the octopus broth. Let boil and add the washed rice, add salt pepper and cook over low fire for 20 minutes, until the rice is cooked.

Remove from the fire, stand for 10 minutes and serve warm.

FRIED SHRIMPS

GARIDES TIGANITES

Preparation time 45 minutes For 4 persons

1 kilo (2 lb, or 36 OZ) shrimps
3 cups olive oil
1 cup beer, 1 cup water
1 egg, salt
1/2 kilo (1 lb, or 18 OZ) flour

OCTOPUS WITH WINE

HTAPODI KRASATO

Preparation time 100 minutes For 4 persons

1 kilo (2 lb, or 36 OZ) octopus
1 cup olive oil
1 onion chopped
1 kilo (2 lb, or 36 OZ) ground ripe tomatoes
2 cups red wine, salt, pepper

STEWED OCTOPUS

HTAPODI STIFADO

Preparation time 145 minutes   For 6 persons

1 1/2 kilo (3 lb, or 54 OZ) octopus
1 1/2 cup olive oil
1 1/2 kilo (3 lb, or 54 OZ) small onions
1 garlic bulb
4 bay leaves
1 kilo (2 lb, or 36 OZ) ground ripe tomatoes
2 cups water
salt and pepper corns

BOILED OCTOPUS

HTAPODI VRASTO

Preparation time 120 minutes

Wash the shrimps very well. Salt them. Dissolve the flour in the water, add the beer and the egg, beaten. Mix to make a thick pap. Put the olive oil in a frying pan to heat. Put some shrimps in the pap and after in the frying pan. Fry of all sides and serve warm with beet-roots or vegetables boiled.

Note: Do not shell the shrimps. You can boil them before frying, without shell them after.

Wash the octopus very well. Cut it in pieces 8 centimeters each. Put it in a saucepan with the olive oil, onion and saute it. Add the wine gradually and cook for 5 minutes. Add the tomatoes, salt and pepper and cook over low fire for 1 hour. During cooking add some water if needed. Serve warm with fried potatoes and season's salad.

Wash the octopus very well and cut it in pieces. Put it in a saucepan with the olive oil, onions (cleaned and washed, not cut) garlic, tomatoes, bay leaves, salt, pepper and cook over low fire for approximately 2 hours, until the octopus is soft and contains a little sauce. If water is needed during cooking, add some. Serve the food warm with fried potatoes.

Wash the octopus very well. Cut it in big pieces and boil it in salted water until soft. Remove its skin and serve it with lemon and olive oil or with vinegar and olive oil, cold. Boiled octopus can accompany other small foods like appetizers. It should not be served as a main dish. See appetizers boiled octopus.

SWEETS
PRESERVES

SPOON SWEETS-MARMALADES-AND COMPOTES

GLYKA KOUTALIOY-MARMELADES-KE KOBOSTES

SOUR CHERRY PRESERVE

VISINO GLYKO

Preparation time about 6 hours

1 1/2 kilo (3 lb, or 54 OZ) sour cherries
1 1/2 kilo (3 lb, or 54 OZ) sugar
1 table spoon lemon juice
300gr. (3/4lb, or 11 OZ) water

QUINCE JAM

KIDONI GLYKO

Preparation time 120 minutes

2 kilos (4lb, or 72 OZ) quince
1 1/2 kilo (3 lb, or 54 OZ) sugar
2 envelopes vanilla
1 table spoon lemon juice
1/2 cup whited almonds
2 cups water

CHERRY PRESERVE

KERASI GLYKO

Preparation time 90 minutes

1 1/2 kilo (3 lb, or 54 OZ) cherries
2 envelopes vanilla
1 1/2 kilo (3 lb, or 54 OZ) sugar
1 table spoon lemon juice
300gr. (3/4lb, or 11 OZ) water

172

Clean the sour cherries of their stems and wash them well. With a hairpin remove the pits without crushing the sour cherries.

Put them in a saucepan and mix them with the sugar. Let them soak for 4 hours, add the water and boil over strong fire. Remove the foam. Boil about 1 hour. When the liquid starts to thicken add the lemon and boil for 3 minutes. Remove from the fire. Let it cool and save. Use it cold anytime you want. For treats or for trimming of creams or icecreams.

Wipe the quince to remove their down. Wash them very well. Peel them. Cut them in thin slices. Cut each slice in oblong pieces. Put them in water. When finish, wash off, and put them in a saucepan with the 2 cups water to boil until soft. Add the sugar and boil them over a very strong fire to thicken the liquid. Add lemon juice, vanilla, and cook for 3 minutes. Remove from the fire. Add the almonds and mix well. The quince must have a golden color. Let it cool and store. Use it as a treat or for trimming on refrigerators cakes.

The cherries must be large and hard. Wash them very well and remove of their stems. With a hairpin remove their pits, being careful not to crush them. Boil the sugar with the water and when it becomes a syrup remove from the fire. Let it cool and add the cherries. Boil them over strong fire until the syrup thickens. Remove the foam, add the lemon juice and cook for 3 minutes more. Remove from the fire and add vanilla. Let it cool and store. Use it as a treat and as a trimming.

APPLE PRESERVE

MILO GLYKO

Preparation time 120 minutes

1 1/2 kilo (3 lb, or 54 OZ) apples
1 kilo (2 lb or 36 OZ) sugar
3 envelopes vanilla
3 cups water
1/2 cup lemon juice

FRESH TOMATO PRESERVE

DOMATAKI GLYKO

1 1/2 kilo (3 lb, or 54 OZ) small seedless tomatoes
1 1/2 kilo (3 lb, or 54 OZ) sugar and
1 kilo (2 lb, or 36 OZ) sugar
3 envelopes vanilla
2 table spoons lemon juice
1 cup water
1/2 cup whited almonds

GRAPE PRESERVE

STAFILI GLYKO

1 1/2 kilo (3 lb, or 54 OZ) grapes
1 kilo (2 lb, or 36 OZ) sugar
2 envelopes vanilla
1 table spoon lemon juice
1 cup water

PEAR PRESERVE

AHLADI GLYKO

1 1/2 kilo (3 lb, or 54 OZ) pears
1 kilo (2 lb, or 36 OZ) sugar
3 cups water
3 envelopes vanilla
1 table spoon lemon juice

The apples must not be very big or very small. Peel them and remove their pits without cutting or breaking the apples. Put them in a saucepan with water and lemon so they will not blacken. Boil the water with the sugar for 10 minutes. Wash off the apples and add them in.

Boil them over strong fire until the syrup thicken. Remove the foam as long as they boil. Add the lemon juice and the vanilla, cook for 10 minutes. Try the syrup and if it is thick, remove from the fire and let cool. Put them in jars and serve cold 1 apple to each person.

The tomatoes must be small, hard and seedless. Wash them well and put in boiling water for 1 minute. Drain and peel them. Add the 1 kilo of sugar and let them soak for 24 hours. The water which drains out of the tomatoes add it in the 1 1/2 kilo of sugar plus 1 cup more (water) and boil for 20 minutes. Put one almond in each tomato and put them in the syrup to boil for 5 minutes. Remove from the fire and let them soak until next day. Next day put on the fire again, add the lemon and boil until the syrup thickens. Add the vanilla and let them cool.

Remove steams of the grapes and wash very well. Put in a saucepan the sugar and water to boil, mixing continuously to dissolve the sugar. When the sugar water thickens to a syrup, add the grapes. Boil over a strong fire for 30 minutes. Add the lemon juice and the vanilla, let for 5 minutes and remove from the fire. Let cool and store in jars.

The pears must be hard. Peel them and throw their pits, without cutting them. Put them in a saucepan with water and lemon so they will not blacken. When done, wash very well. Put them in a saucepan with the water and the sugar to boil over low fire until very soft. Remove from the fire and let them stand for 24 hours. Put on the fire again, add the lemon and let them boil until the syrup thickens. Add the vanilla and allow to cool, and store.

FRESH FIG MARMALADE

SYKO MARMELADA

1 1/2 kilo (3 lb, or 54 OZ) fresh figs
750gr. (1 3/4lb, or 27 OZ) sugar

APRICOT MARMALADE

VERIKOKO MARMELADA

1 1/2 kilo (3 lb, or 54 OZ) apricots
1 1/2 kilo (3 lb, or 54 OZ) sugar
1 cup water

APPLE MARMALADE

MILO MARMELADA

1 1/2 kilo (3 lb, or 54 OZ) apples
1 kilo (2 lb, or 36 OZ) sugar
2 cups water

PEAR MARMALADE
AHLADI MARMELADA
1 1/2 kilo (3 lb, or 54 OZ) pears
1 kilo (2 lb, or 36 OZ) sugar
2 cups water

APPLE COMPOTE

MILO KOBOSTA

1 kilo (2 lb, or 36 OZ) very hard apples
3 cups water
2 cups sugar
peel of one lemon
1 stick of cinnamon

The figs must be ripe. Peel them and pulpify with your hands. Put them in a saucepan with the sugar. Boil them until the marmalade separates from the spoon and falls like a thick mass. Remove from the fire, let it cool and store in jars.

The apricots must be ripe. Wash them and remove the pits. Boil them with the water for 45 minutes and grind. Put their pulp with the sugar and boil over strong fire. Mix continuously so that the marmalade will not stick in the saucepan. When it starts to fall from the ladle like a thick mass, it is ready. Remove from the fire, let it cool and store in jars.

The apples must be ripe. Peel them and remove their pits. Put them in a saucepan with water and lemon juice, so not to blacken. Wash off and boil with the 2 cups water until dissolved. Grind them, and their pulp, put it with the sugar to boil over strong fire. When the marmalade thicknens and falls from the ladle, remove from the fire, let cool and store in jars.

These are made exactly like the apple marmalade.

Peel the apples and cut them in half. Remove their pits and put them in a saucepan with water and lemon, so not to blacken. When finished, wash off, and boil with the sugar and water. Add the lemon's peel and cinnamon. Pierce the apples with a fork and if they are soft, remove from the fire and take them out ot the syrup. Boil the syrup to thicken, remove the cinnamon and lemon's peel and baste the apples with it. Let them cool and store in jars.

PEAR COMPOTE

AHLADI KOBOSTA

1 kilo (2 lb, or 36 OZ) hard pears

1 1/2 cup water
1 1/2 cup sugar
the peel of one lemon
1 envelope vanilla

PEACH COMPOTE

RODAKINO KOBOSTA

1 kilo (2 lb, or 36 OZ) hard peaches
1 cup water
1 1/2 cup sugar

MIXED COMPOTE

ANAMIKTI KOBOSTA

4 pears
4 peaches
6 apples
6 apricots
2 sticks of cinnamon
2 cups sugar
2 cups water
5 cloves
the peel of one lemon

COOKIES-PASTRIES-AND CAKES

VANILLA COOKIES

KOULOURAKIA VANILIAS

Preparation time 120 minutes

1 1/2 kilo (3 lb, or 54 OZ) flour
6 eggs
1/2 kilo (1 lb, or 18 OZ) sugar

1 1/2 cup butter
1 cup milk
5 envelopes vanilla
2 tea spoons bicarbonate of ammonia
1 tea spoon baking powder

These are made exactly like the apple compote. But before you take them out of the syrup add the vanilla.

Wash the peaches and peel them. Open them in the middle and remove their pit. Put in water with lemon, so not to blacken. Wash off. Put them in a sauce pan with the sugar and water to boil until soft. (Pierce them with a fork, if soft they are done). As soon as soft take them out of the syrup. Continue to boil the syrup until thick. Remove from the fire and let it half cool. Baste the peaches, let cool and store in the refrigerator.

Peal the pears and the apples and remove their pits. Cut them in small cubes and put them in a saucepan with lemon and water. Peel the peaches, cut them in small cubes, add them in the water and lemon. Wash and cut in cubes the apricots and put in the water with lemon, also. Wash off the apples and pears and put in a saucepan with the sugar, water, cloves, cinnamon and the lemon's peel to boil for 10 minutes. Add the peaches (washed off) and boil for 10 more minutes. Wash off the apricots, add them in too. After 10 minutes boiling, drain all the fruits. Discard cinnamon, cloves, lemon's peel, and put on the fire again until the syrup is thick. Remove from the fire and when half cool baste the fruits with juice. Let all cool and store in jars in the refrigerator.

Mix the flour with the baking powder. Warm the milk and dissolve the ammonia in it. Beat the eggs very well. Add in, the vanilla and sugar. Beat the butter until creamy. Put the butter in the beaten eggs with the sugar, mix for 3 minutes, add the milk with the ammonia. Mix for 3 more minutes add the flour. Mix very well to make a soft paste. Shape small round cookies and lay them in a greased baking pan. Coat with 1 beaten egg and bake in medium oven for 20 minutes.

COOKIES WITH CINNAMON

KOULOURAKIA ME KANELA

Preparation time 120 minutes

1 1/4 of kilo (1 1/2 lb, or 45 OZ) flour
4 eggs
1 1/2 cup sugar
1 cup butter
1 cup milk
1 tea spoon ground cloves
2 tea spoons bicarbonate of ammonia
1 table spoon cinnamon powder

BISCUITS WITH BUTTER

BISKOTA VOUTIROY

Preparation time 180 minutes

4 cups flour
1 1/2 cup sugar
3/4 of cup butter
5 eggs
2 envelopes vanilla
3/4 of cup chopped white almonds
2 tea spoons baking powder

BISCUITS WITH CHOCOLATE

BISKOTA SOKOLATAS

Preparation time 145 minutes

4 cups flour
1 1/2 cup sugar
1/2 cup cocoa
3/4 of cup butter
1/3 of cup warm milk
4 eggs
3 tea spoons baking powder
3 envelopes vanilla

Dissolve the ammonia in warm milk. Beat separately the yolks from the whites. Beat the whites very well until stiff. Beat the yolks with the sugar very well. Grind the cloves to be like powder and mix them with cinnamon and flour. Add the flour in a bowl and put in the melt butter, mixing them well. Add the milk with ammonia, the yolks with sugar, the whites and knead to make a soft paste. Shape cookies in any form you want and lay them in an oily baking pan. Coat with beaten egg and bake in medium oven for 20 minutes.

Mix the flour with baking powder. Beat the eggs, add vanilla in. Cream the butter, add sugar in and mix well. Add the eggs in butter. Add the flour gradually and make a soft paste. Cover it with greased foil and let it stand for half an hour. Knead again. Take some paste and make a sheet (phyllo) 1 inch thick. Cut it with a biscuit cutter and lay the biscuits in a greased baking pan. Coat them with beaten egg and add chopped almonds. Bake in hot oven for 15 minutes.

Beat the eggs with vanilla very well. Mix the half cup sugar with cocoa to dissolve it in milk. Mix the flour with baking powder. Cream the butter. Add in it, the one cup sugar and continue mixing. Add the eggs with vanilla, milk, in which you have dissolved cocoa very well, add sugar and mix very well. Add the flour gradually and knead to make a soft paste. Take some paste and open a sheet (phyllo) 1 inch thickness. Cut it in differents forms and lay them in a greased baking pan. Bake in very hot oven for 10 minutes.

GREEK EASTER COOKIES

TSOUREKIA PASHALINA

Preparation time 120 minutes

750gr. (1 3/4lb, or 27 OZ) flour
4 eggs
2 envelopes vanilla
1 tea spoon bicarbonate of ammonia
1 cup sugar
1/3 of cup milk
1 cup butter

GREEK COOKIES WITH ALMONDS

KOURABIEDES ME AMIGDALO

Preparation time 180 minutes

750gr. (1 3/4lb, or 27 OZ) confectioner's sugar
2 egg yolks
2 envelopes vanilla
2 cups fresh butter
5 cups flour
1/2 cup sugar
2 cups white roasted almonds
1 tea spoon baking powder
1 cup rose-water

GREEK COOKIES WITH HONEY

MELOMAKARONA

Preparation time 180 minutes

750gr. (1 3/4lb, or 27 OZ) soft flour (as much as needed)
200gr. (1/2 lb, or 7 OZ) sugar
250gr. (3/4lb, or 9 OZ) olive oil
200gr. (1/2 lb, or 7 OZ) orange and lemon juice
250gr. (3/4lb, or 9 OZ) chopped walnuts
1/2 cup cognac (brandy)
2 tea spoons baking powder

Syrup:
500gr. (1 lb, 18 OZ) honey
250gr. (1/2 lb, or 9 OZ) water

Warm the milk and dissolve in it, the ammonia. Beat the eggs well and melt the butter. Put the flour in a bowl and add the melt butter, eggs, vanilla, sugar and the milk, in it. Mix all the ingredients well to make a soft paste. Shape with your hands a cord 1 centimeter thick and fold it 3 times in any form you want. Round or oblong. Put the tsourekia in an oily baking pan, coat them with 1 beaten egg and bake in medium oven for 20 minutes.

Boil the almonds for 10 minutes and peel them. Roast them lightly. Mix the flour with baking powder and vanilla. Cream the butter, add sugar, yolks and continue mixing. Add the almonds and flour gradually. Knead very well and shape kourabiedes in the form you want. Lay them in a greased baking pan and bake in a warm oven (medium) for 20 minutes. Remove them from the oven sprinkle with the rose water and coat with the confectioner sugar. If you want, do not use the almonds.

Mix the flour with baking powder. Mix the sugar with olive oil for 45 minutes about. Add the walnuts, orange and lemon juice, cognac and mix well. Gradually add the flour, mix all together and make a soft paste. Shape into cylindrical forms, push them at the top with your palm, and lay them in a greased baking pan. Baked them in warm medium oven for 30 minutes about.

In a saucepan put the honey with water to boil. Remove from the oven and let them cool. Dip them in the honey. Remove with a ladle having holes and put over them the walnuts and some cinnamon.

CAKE WITH RAISINS AND WALNUTS

KEIK ME STAFIDES KE KARIDIA

Preparation time 120 minutes

4 eggs
3 cups flour
1 1/2 cup sugar
1/2 cup warm milk
1 cup butter
1/2 cup chopped walnuts
1/2 cup chopped raisins
2 envelopes vanilla
3 tea spoons baking powder

ALMOND OR WALNUT STUFFED PASTRY ROLLS

FLOYERES ME AMYGDALA I KARIDIA

Preparation time 2 1/2 hours

Stuffing:

750gr. (1 3/4 lb or 27 OZ) baklava phyllo leaves
2 1/2 cups almonds or walnuts crumbs
1/2 cup toast bread crumbs
3/4 of cup sugar
2 eggs
1 tea spoon cinnamon powder
butter or oil for the baklava phyllo leaves

Syrup:

2 1/2 cups water
3 1/2 cups sugar
the peel of 1 lemon and 1 tea spoon lemon juice
1 stick of cinnamon

HALVAS WITH SEMOLINA

HALVAS ME SIMIGDALI

Preparation time 45 minutes

500gr (1 lb, or 18 OZ) thin semolina
1 cup flour   3 cups sugar
1 1/2 cup olive oil   1 liter water

Mix the flour with baking powder and vanilla. Wash the raisins and chopped them. Crush the walnuts in a mortar. Add the raisins and walnuts in the flour. Beat the egg whites until creamy. Cream the butter with the sugar and add in, the yolks, milk, flour and egg whites. Mix very well. Add the mixture in a greased cake pan and bake in medium oven for 1 hour. Let it cool and remove from the pan.

Crush the almonds and the toast bread. Mix them together. Mix the eggs, sugar, cinnamon and almond crumbs. Melt the butter for the phyllo leaves. Take each leaf, oil it, cut it in three pieces and lay some mixture at the tip.

Fold the sides to inside and roll it. Butter the floyera. Lay them in a greased baking pan, sprinkle with some water and bake in medium oven for 15 minutes. Boil the water, sugar, cinnamon, lemon's peel and juice for 15 minutes. When take out of the oven the floyeres let them cool. Pierce them with a fork and dip in very hot syrup. With the syrup left over, baste all around the floyeres.

Boil the water and sugar until it is syrup. Heat the olive oil very much, add semolina and flour in. Lower fire and mix continuously to lightly brown.

Add syrup and continue mixing until it is a thick dough. Put it in a cake form, let it cool and put it in the refrigerator. Serve when chilled.

VANILLA CREAM PIE

GALAKTOBOUREKO

Preparation time 2 1/2 hours

Cream:
3 table spoons fresh butter
1 kilo (2 lb, or 36 OZ) milk
5 eggs
1/2 kilo (1 lb, or 27 OZ) baklava phyllo leaves
1 1/2 cup sugar
1/2 cup butter for the leaves
1 cup ground semolina
2 envelopes vanilla

Syrup:

2 1/2 cups water
3 1/2 cups sugar
1 tea spoon lemon juice and
the peel of 1 lemon

NUT FILLED KADAIFI

KADAIFI

Preparation time 2 hours and 40 minutes

Stuffing:
750gr. (1 3/4 lb, or 27 OZ) kadaifi pastry sheets (phyllo)
2 eggs
1 cup butter
2 1/2 cups almond crumbs
1 tea spoon cinnamon powder
3 table spoons sugar

Syrup:

2 1/2 cups water
3 1/2 cups sugar
1 stick of cinnamon
the peel of one lemon and 1 tea
spoon lemon juice

NEW YEAR'S CAKE

VASILOPITTA

Preparation time 1 1/2 hour

250gr. (1/2 lb, or 9 OZ) butter
1 kilo (2 lb, or 36 OZ) flour
1/2 kilo (1 lb, or 18 OZ) sugar
8 eggs
1 cup cognac

1 tea spoon baking soda
the juice of 6 oranges
2 tea spoons baking powder
1 tea spoon grated orange peel

Heat the milk, add semolina mixing continuously until thick. Re—
move from the fire. Beat the eggs and add sugar and vanilla, mixing
all the time. Add butter and mix it until dissolved. When cream cools
grease a medium size baking pan. Butter each one the half leaves, lay
them in the baking pan and put over them the cream. Fold the sides
to inside, butter them and lay over them the rest half leaves butter
each one. Cut the leaves which protrude, brush the top with butter,
sprinkle with water.

Bake in medium oven for half an hour.

Boil the water, sugar, lemon juice and lemon peel for 15 minutes.
After galaktoboureko is done, pour over syrup.

Boil the almonds for 10 minutes, peel and crush them. Mix them
with the cinnamon, sugar and eggs. Melt the butter. Open some phyllo kadaifi and lay at the tip one table spoon almonds. Roll it tightly to
enclose the stuffing and lay it in a greased baking pan. With a tea spoon take some melted butter and coat the kadaifi. Do like this until all
the stuff, finish. Bake in medium oven for half an hour.

Boil the sugar, water, cinnamon, juice and the peel of lemon for 25
minutes. As the kadaifi will be hot, coat it with syrup. Let it cool and
serve.

Squeeze the oranges and dissolve in them, baking soda. Beat the
whites till creamy. Cream the butter. Add in to the yolks, sugar and
mix well. Add the orange juice, cognac, and mix continuously. Mix the
flour with baking powder and orange scrapings. Add in, some egg
whites, some flour until finished. Mix all ingredients well until it is a
thick batter. Grease a baking pan, add the mixture. Bake in medium
oven for 1 hour. Let it cool and serve.

Note: This cake is made in Greece and is offered the first day of
each new year, which is how the cake acquired its name.

MENU

Pastry with roguefort cheese
Potato balls
Chicken salad
Onion soup
Mixed souvlakia
Spinach with rice
Apple compote

Fried liver of lamb or beef
Meat salad
Fried squash
Vegetable soup
Fried pork steaks
Baked potatoes with cumin
Vanilla cream pie

Appetizer with eggs and cheese
Baked potatoes
Cabbage and carrot salad
Spinach soup
Stuffed chicken
Baked mashed spinach
Pear compote

Appetizer with crab
Boiled octopus
Cheese rolls
Beer soup
Fish souvlakia
Shrimp salad
Mixed compote

Stuffed grapevine leaves
Boiled cauliflower salad
Vegetable soup
Boiled veal
Vegetables with pilaf
Pear compote

Fried meat balls
Village salad
Baked macaroni
Loaf with ground meat
Mushrooms with olive oil
Almond baklave

Cheese for ouzo
Lettuce salad
Baked macaroni with minced meat
Cheese rolls
Refrigerated orange cake

Appetizers with eggs and cheese
Tomato and cucumber salad
Potato, squash, eggplant mousaka
Season's fruit
Melon of ice

Codfish croquettes
Fried squid
Garlic sauce
Fried dried codfish
Beet-root salad
Nut filled kadaifi

Cheese for ouzo
Potato balls
Partridge in the oven
Vegetables with pilaf
Banana of ice

Rice soup avgolemono
Stuffed turkey
Cabbage and carrot salad
Cheese
Vanilla cream pie

Bean soup
Souvlakia with sausages
Eggs stuffed
Cheese
Lettuce salad
Apple loaf

Spinach rice
Fried cuttlefish
Shrimp salad
Cheese
Apple compote

Fried squid
Baked eggs with spinach
Village salad
Cheese
Mixed compote

Snails with onions stew
Potato balls
Artichoke salad
Cheese
Lemon of ice

String beans with olive oil
Grilled fish
Potato balls
Cheese
Semolina cake

Eggplants imam bayldi
Boiled octopus
Cabbage and carrot salad
Season's fruit
Cream

Filled eggplants little shoes
Fried cuttle fish
Tomato and cucumber salad
Season's fruit
Melon of ice

Boiled veal
Tomato soup with vermicelli
Meat salad
Cheese
Refrigerated orange cake

Meat balls with egg and lemon sauce
Pastry with roquefort cheese
Village salad
Baked apples

Chick-pea soup
Fried squid
Boiled cauliflower salad
Mixed compote

Pork with celery and egg and lemon sauce
Baked pilaf
Village salad
Baked quince

GREEK COFFEE

KAFES ELINIKOS

Strong and sweet-varis glykos

1 demitasse cup (very small cup) of water
1 1/2 tea spoon sugar
1 tea spoon powdered coffee

Medium strong with little sugar-metrios

1 demitasse cup (very small cup) water
1 tea spoon sugar
1 1/2 tea spoon powdered coffee

Without sugar-sketos

1 demitasse cup (very small cup) water
1 tea spoon powdered coffee

Put the water in a small pot, add sugar and coffee. Mix to dissolve the sugar and coffee and boil to the top of the pot. Remove from the fire and serve the coffee immediately in demitasse cups.